RAYS *of the* SAME LIGHT

Volume One

RAYS *of the* SAME LIGHT

PARALLEL PASSAGES, WITH COMMENTARY, FROM THE BIBLE AND THE BHAGAVAD GITA

—— Volume One ——

J. Donald Walters

Crystal Clarity, Publishers
14618 Tyler Foote Road
Nevada City, CA 95959

Cover design by Bella Potapovskaya
Cover photo by J. Donald Walters

This work is lovingly dedicated
to my great spiritual teacher,
Paramhansa Yogananda

Other books by the same author:

Contents

Part III — *The Soul's Ascent*

Introduction to
Volume One

Christianity, for the first thousand years of its existence, was far more mystically inclined than it has been these past few centuries. Hermits withdrew to desert solitudes by the thousands to devote their lives to prayer and meditation. Monks and nuns entered cloisters with the deep hope of communing with God. A life lived in unceasing prayer was held in universal esteem.

Early Church literature is filled with mystical accounts of visions and miracles. Inner communion with God was ardently sought outside the monasteries as well as inside them.

The faith of people in those first centuries was relatively simple. It hadn't yet become all tangled up, as it is now, with sectarian differences, and with scholarly debates based on archeological finds, and with worries as to whether God was male or (to use a word that is heard nowadays in theological debates) bisexual, and with carefully worded concessions to the spiritual skepticism of a scientific era.

It wouldn't have occurred to those early Christians to explain away the miracles of Christ, as so many writers do now. Surely it is only this Twentieth Century that could have given rise to the description — offered no doubt in the sincere hope of saving Christendom itself — of the miracle of the loaves and fishes as a triumph of Christian charity.

For Jesus, so a modern author has explained, realized that many of those present that day had brought no food to eat. Lovingly, therefore, he divided with those near him whatever loaves and fishes he had with him in his own hamper. Inspired by his example, all those others with food baskets of their own also began sharing their meals with others. And so, all the five thousand were fed.

This is an excellent teaching, no doubt — except that it leaves one wondering if, just maybe, none of those other miracles of Jesus actually happened, either. And if not, maybe what he said was never actually said.

In fact, the debate has been raging for decades, if not for several centuries, as to whether Jesus even lived.

An English churchman even went that debate one better some years back, with the announcement: "God is dead."

I took part in a religious forum in London a few years ago. The speaker prior to me was a dean of the Church of England. The essence of his diatribe (and that, I'm afraid, is essentially what it was) he himself expressed with the shouted declaration: "We must politicize religion!"

If he was angry before, he was furious afterwards. For with all respect I simply couldn't let his speech stand as given. In a few words I told the audience, "If you feel inspired by God to express your religion politically, then by all means do so. But don't accept that you *must* do anything of the sort without such inspiration. It would be just as holy an act for you to sweep up leaves in the park, if that is what God inspires you to do."

There isn't much talk these days of being inspired by God from within. And there has been altogether too much talk of rejecting any such inspiration; of having nothing to do with the inspired feelings that come to one in prayer and meditation; even of leaving God out of one's reckoning altogether, and concentrating entirely on social service, good deeds, and the like, with the excuse that "The proper concern of mankind is man."

Many insist that Jesus was a social reformer, and not a mystic at all.

Frank Laubach, the great missionary and modern mystic, launched a campaign a few years ago to get more ministers in American churches simply to mention God in their sermons.

But if those early Christians had another view of Christianity altogether, isn't it possible that theirs was the right one — assuming, of course, that Jesus himself knew what he was supposed to be teaching. They lived much closer to his times. It might be possible for us to refine what they believed, but surely it is presumptuous of people in this remote age so flagrantly to contradict it.

Inner communion with God was essential to the belief of early Christians. Heaven, through the redeeming power of Christ's death on the cross, was always men's hope for the future, but God was also for them a very present reality. Most revered among mankind, moreover, were those saints who lived consciously in His presence within.

And this is the purpose of this book. My hope is to awaken Christians to the awareness that when Jesus spoke to the woman of Samaria of "living water," he was offering her a *present* experience of God's love, joy, and peace. *This* was the "good news" of the Gospels. It was to inner communion with God that Jesus was calling all those "who had ears to hear."

Preface
to Volume One

These commentaries were written to be studied in pairs, one pair for every week of the year. The present volume covers the first four months of the year.

I presented these commentaries in sets of two because it is my hope to show that the great teachings of the ages are not dogmas, merely, but universal truths.

Selections from the greatest Scripture of the East, the Bhagavad Gita, are offered to lend fresh emphasis to parallel teachings in the Bible.

It happens in human conversation as well: Often, when a concept has been re-worded, it is suddenly perceived in a new light.

Similarly, if we hear how another great Scripture has worded teachings that are familiar to us in the Bible, we may understand them more fully. For any great truth, like a great temple, is many sided. Too long a familiarity with only one side may cause us to overlook the others. Too long an exposure, similarly, to one interpretation of the teachings of Jesus may blind us to the possibility of other meanings. In this sense, comparison with passages from the Bhagavad Gita will, I believe, give readers a deeper understanding of the Holy Bible as well.

The quotations in these pages derive from a number of different translations, both of the Bible and of the Bhagavad Gita. Where poetry seemed more important than prosaic exactitude, I generally used the beautiful King James translation of the Bible, and Sir Edwin Arnold's inspiring poetic rendition of the Bhagavad Gita. Otherwise, I compared the various texts available, and selected those which I thought gave them the clearest meaning, or which were the easiest to read — altering a word or two, occasionally, only to enhance their beauty.

****

A few words as to the genesis of these commentaries:

They are based on the teachings of the great contemporary mystic, Paramhansa Yogananda. Yogananda was sent to America in 1920 by his line of spiritual teachers. Here he remained for the remaining thirty-two years of his life.

During those years, he wrote a number of books, trained many disciples, and founded an internationally respected organization: Self-Realization Fellowship, with its headquarters in Los Angeles, California.

Chief among the books he authored is one that has become a spiritual classic of our times: *Autobiography of a Yogi,* a work which has been translated into numerous languages.

Yogananda has gained renown throughout the world as one of the great spiritual figures of our times. Indeed, countless thousands, both within and outside his circle of followers, revere him as a true saint.

Part of his mission on earth was to help people to understand the original teachings of Jesus in the New Testament, and of Krishna in the Bhagavad Gita, and to show the underlying compatibility of those two teachings.

Such, then, has been also my purpose in writing this book.

I had the good fortune to live with Paramhansa Yogananda during the last several years of his life, until his passing in 1952. I worked with him on his writings, and received also from him personally — and not only in written form — the teachings that will be found in these pages.

I had the further good fortune of lecturing on his behalf for three years as his representative. For many years since then I have continued to teach, both in America and around the world, and to make his teachings better known.

Paramhansa Yogananda empowered me to do a particular work: the founding of a spiritual community, to which I gave the name "Ananda."

Ananda has grown and flourished over the past twenty years to become what Yogananda long envisioned — truly a World Brotherhood Village, with resident members from many countries.

More than forty years have passed since I first came to Yogananda, and became his disciple. During all this time I have meditated profoundly on how to explain as simply and clearly as possible for people of Western upbringing the depth and subtlety of his Scriptural commentaries.

This present volume represents my first attempt to offer in detail the fruit of those meditations.

It is my humble prayer that this endeavor will be of some service, both to my great teacher and his earthly mission, and to the reader, whose desire, I hope, is to understand the Scriptures more deeply.

Part I

The Eternal Christ

At The Heart of Silence: The Eternal "Word"

Bible

What Is the "Word"?

This passage is from the Gospel of St. John, Chapter 1, Verses 1-5:

"In the beginning was the Word, and the Word was with God, and the Word was God. The same was in the beginning with God. All things were made by him; and without him was not any thing made that was made. In him was life; and the life was the light of men. And the light shineth in darkness; and the darkness comprehended it not."

Commentary

The Gospel of St. Matthew begins with a genealogy of Jesus. The Gospel of St. Mark begins with an account of John the Baptist as the herald for Jesus' mission on earth. St. Luke's Gospel begins with the story of the birth of Jesus, and the miraculous events preceding it. Only St. John's Gospel presents us from the beginning with the mystical importance of Jesus' birth: the descent of the Infinite Christ, and its manifestation on earth in human form for the redemption of mankind.

Of the four Gospels, St. John's is the deepest, spiritually. Its constant emphasis is on Jesus in his divine aspect, as distinct from Jesus in his humanity; on Jesus in his eternal reality as the Son of God, rather than in his fleeting earthly manifestation as the son of man.

St. John gives us at the outset one of the most profoundly mystical passages in the Bible. What is meant here by the Word? Many learned texts have been written on the subject. Countless pious debates over the centuries have centered in the theological niceties of the Word as a person, or as an emanation, or as a Platonic concept as opposed to a Hebrew one.

In matters of this spiritual depth, to expect intellectually guided theologians to bring light into the dark waters of mystical truths is like expecting a diver to shed light in the ocean depths with a candle.

Medieval maps described uncharted regions of the earth with fantastic phrases, such as: "Here be griffins." People traveling too far at sea were once imagined sailing over the earth's edge into nothingness. (How, one wonders, did they imagine that the waters themselves were contained?) Travelers who claimed to have visited distant regions were dismissed airily when the tales they brought back didn't correspond to popular fantasy. Indeed, for centuries people would say, "What a Marco Polo!"

meaning, "What a lie!"

Only as adventurers began to voyage in greater numbers into the unknown, and to corroborate one another's stories, did people begin to believe their descriptions of uncharted regions, and to insist on reports based on actual experience rather than on fantasy.

In spiritual realms, also, so long as the "experts" respected by most people are the theologians, and so long as direct mystical experience is viewed with suspicion or dismissed as "subjective," we have a situation aptly described by Jesus as "the blind leading the blind."

Those alone with divine experience have a right to explain the nature of divine experience.

Thus, as St. John begins his Gospel at the very summit of its message, so let us begin at the highest level of our own authority for what these Scripture commentaries contain. Cutting through the Gordian knot of intellectual debate, we state, simply, that what follows is the explanation of one of the spiritual giants of our time.

The levels of spiritual truth that Paramhansa Yogananda described were not an unknown territory, never reported on before. His genius, in fact, lay in showing how the reports of all great saints, however obscurely they may have expressed themselves, coincided in every essential. His genius lay also in his ability to make the subtlest mystical realms somehow real to our imaginations. For it was in the language of every day that he described what he had experienced. He never left his students bemused with poetic symbolism, the purpose of which is often rather to hint than to reveal.

The genius of his writing and teaching, indeed, was its crystal clarity.

Yogananda was a master: one, that is to say, who had attained God-realization, and who spoke as Jesus did when he said, "We speak that which we do know, and testify that which we have seen." (John 3:11) Basing his teaching on direct inner communion with God and with Christ, he showed also that in numerous ancient traditions there exist corollaries for his explanation of the Word.

His explanation was stated in amazingly simple terms, easy to understand. The Bible, indeed, uses words to suggest familiar concepts to our minds, and not to confound our understanding. In speaking of the Word, the purpose is to draw some kind of parallel to human speech.

What is speech? It is the intelligent expression of thought. It is, in other words, thought made manifest. It is a vibration of sound, uttered not only to communicate, but also to initiate action.

The Word of God, similarly, is the creative vibration of His consciousness. It is a wordless manifestation of sound, resulting from the vibration of God's intelligence in its process of producing His vast creation.

Modern physics tells us that the atoms, from which all things are made, are in a state of constant vibration. Vibration differs from simple movement in its repeated reference to a central point: like the tines of a tuning fork, which move left and right from a point of rest in the center; or like the ocean waves, which rise and fall without changing the over-all level of the water.

A part of God's consciousness, similarly, vibrated from its center of absolute peace, and produced the appearance of a manifested universe, even as an ocean seems at the surface to be an infinity of heaving waves, instead of a vast, unchanging body of water.

In the beginning, we read in Genesis 1:2, "The earth was without form, and void; and darkness was upon the face of the deep." God, the Father, existed as pure Spirit: ever-existing, ever-conscious, ever-new Bliss. When the Lord decided to create, so we read again in Genesis, "The Spirit of God moved upon the face of the waters."

The movement of God's spirit "upon the face of the waters" is the infinite creative vibration: the Amen of the Book of Revelation; the Aum of Hindu yogis; the Ahunavar of the ancient Zoroastrians. It is God's own consciousness in vibratory movement. Therefore the Word not only proceeds from God: It is God. All things were made by it; nor, without it (as the Bible says), was any thing made that was made.

Thus, through the Holy Bible, God has spoken to mankind.

Bhagavad Gita

God Is the One Reality

This passage is from the seventh Chapter, the 6th and 7th Stanzas:

"I make and unmake this universe. Apart from Me nothing exists, O Arjuna. All things, like the beads of a necklace, are strung together on the thread of My consciousness, and are sustained by Me."

Commentary

In this reading the Bhagavad Gita explains the mystery of Cosmic Creation. All that exists is a manifestation of God's own consciousness. It was dreamed by Him into existence. The atoms of creation form part of that dream. Like the thread passing through a necklace, the divine consciousness runs through all things. It unites seemingly diverse phenomena in a single, changeless reality.

There is a difference between God's creation and His indwelling presence in creation. God is equally present in everything — no more so in the greatest star than in the smallest atom. It was, indeed, His consciousness that actually became the star and the atom. He dreamed the universe into existence. Nor was there anything but His consciousness, in the beginning, out of which to create anything.

While the universe is a manifestation of God, in which sense God may be said to be the universe, this doesn't in any way mean that He is defined by His creation, or limited to it, any more than a dreamer's reality is limited to his dream. Nor does it mean that universal creation is conscious of the indwelling Lord, whom it manifests.

The task before us, indeed, as created beings, is to become conscious of Him as our own deepest reality; to realize Him, hidden in the depths of our being, beneath the restless waves of our unceasing thoughts, desires, and ego-directed ambitions.

The Lord ever calls to us to probe beneath the surface of superficial appearances: always, even at the heart of life's storms, to find Him, the unchanging Spirit.

This inner communion with the Lord is the essence of religion. It is, above all, what great masters like Krishna and Jesus came on earth to teach to humanity.

Thus, therefore, through the Bhagavad Gita, God has spoken to mankind.

Did God *Create* the Universe? Or Did He *Become* it?

Bible

Our Eternal Heritage

This passage is from the Gospel of St. John, Chapter 1, Verses 4 and 5:

"In him was life; and the life was the light of men. And the light shineth in darkness; and the darkness comprehended it not."

Commentary

The Bible is saying here that in the Word of God was life. This reference to life, as previously to the Word itself, is profoundly mystical. For as the life of man is not his body, but that which animates his body, so the life of the universe is that which eternally animates and sustains it: the indwelling Spirit of God.

It was to this true, divine life that Jesus was referring when he said, in John 10:10, "I am come that they might have life, and that they might have it more abundantly." The life of which he was speaking was not sentience, merely. He spoke of human life without God, indeed, as a form of living death. His references to true life were always to the divine life within man.

St. John's Gospel begins with the statement that universal creation was brought into manifestation by the power of the Word: "In the beginning was the Word, and the Word was with God, and the Word was God." This Word, or divine creative vibration, is different from creation itself, just as the pot is different from the potter. The Word is God in that aspect of His consciousness which manifests and sustains His creation. It is at that level of reality that the divine life exists of which the Gospel speaks.

Vibration of any kind produces two manifestations: sound, and light. God's Cosmic Vibration is here described as the Word, because sound, in the form of words, gives utterance to human thought. Even so, God's Word gives utterance, or outward manifestation, to His ideas for creation.

The Book of Genesis, on the other hand, emphasizes the other aspect of Cosmic Vibration: Light. As we read there, "And God said, Let there be light: and there was light." (Genesis 1:3) That is why also St. John wrote, in this first chapter of his Gospel, "And the life was the light of men." All that which is light in us, and that which leads us forward into ever greater light, comes to us from God, never from mere affirmation, study and philosophy.

Many great saints have communed with God as

both Sound and Light. As we read in Ezekiel 43:1,2: "Afterward he brought me to the gate, even the gate that looketh toward the east: And, behold, the glory of the God of Israel came from the way of the east: and his voice was like a noise of many waters: and the earth shined with his glory."

The abstract aspects of truth — such as how God manifested His universe — are less immediately important to us than the question of how we ourselves might grow closer to God. The essential thing to understand, then, is that God, in His aspects of Sound and Light, can be perceived by mankind in deep inner silence.

By deep inner communion with the Word of God — the Holy Ghost, as Jesus also called it — whether as Sound or Light, we can reclaim our eternal heritage in the Lord. Instruction on how to commune with these subtle realities forms an important part of true spiritual teachings.

Deep beneath the waves of your human restlessness, seek communion with the Supreme Lord, whose kingdom, as Jesus said, is within you.

For thus, through the Holy Bible, God has spoken to mankind.

Bhagavad Gita

The World Is a Dream of God's

This passage is from the seventh Chapter, the 8th through the 10th Stanzas:

"I am the fluidity of water. I am the silver light of the moon and the golden light of the sun. I am the Aum chanted in all the vedas: the Cosmic Sound moving as if soundlessly through the ether. I am the manliness of men. I am the good sweet smell of the moist earth. I am the luminescence of fire; the sustaining life of all living creatures. I am self-offering in those who would expand their little lives into cosmic life. O Arjuna, know Me as the eternal seed of all creatures. In the perceptive, I am their perception. In the great, I am their greatness. In the glorious, it is I who am their glory."

Commentary

Wise is the person who in all things beholds God as the Doer: who gives to God the glory for all that he does well; and who sees in his every failure the failure only of his perfect attunement to the Lord.

Wise is he who in all things sees the hand of God: who, in laughter, sees God's smile; and in sorrow, sees the tenderness of God's reproach.

For the world is a dream of God's. The appointed task of mankind is to awaken from the cosmic dream, and to live in conscious communion with Him by Whom and from Whom the dream was produced.

God, in this passage of the Bhagavad Gita, is saying not only, "I am in the water, the moon," etc., but, "I am the water, the moon, and each and every thing that exists." It would be easy to conclude from these words that things in themselves are divine. It was in this error that idol worship became a sin. For when we love the creation more than the Creator, we become trapped in pettiness, and forget who we really are: the children of the Lord.

What we must do is love all things in God's name. There is nothing wrong with seeing God in the clouds at sunset, and in a burst of sunlight through the treetops; with hearing His divine melodies through the songs of birds, and feeling His power in the blowing of the wind. But those who look to these manifestations for their inspiration, and forget the deeper Reality expressed in these things, sin against their own highest potential.

Things are divine not for their beauty — after all,

not everything is equally beautiful, whereas God's presence is equally everywhere! — but for the fact that, locked in the heart of each of them, may be found some Godly message, some truth, some divine inspiration.

The rocks convey a message of steadfastness. The honey bee tells us wordlessly to sip only sweetness, not filth. The clouds offer an example of aloofness from petty earthly preoccupations, while offering their help impartially to all through the rain.

Behind everything we see, let us look ever to God's unseen presence.

Thus, through the Bhagavad Gita, God has spoken to mankind.

Where There Is Ignorance, Is God Present?

Bible

"The Light Shineth in Darkness"

This passage is from the Gospel of St. John, Chapter 1, Verses 1-5:

"In the beginning was the Word, and the Word was with God, and the Word was God. The same was in the beginning with God. All things were made by him; and without him was not any thing made that was made. In him was life; and the life was the light of men. And the light shineth in darkness, and the darkness comprehended it not."

Commentary

In the past weeks we have considered the first four of these Verses. Let us now consider the last:

"And the light shineth in darkness, and the darkness comprehended it not."

How is it possible for the divine light to shine in darkness and yet make no impression on it — not even, as the Bible puts it, to be "comprehended" by it? Ordinarily, light and darkness exist in dynamic relationship to each other. The struggle between God's light on the one hand, and the darkness of evil on the other, provides one of the classic themes of spiritual literature. Yet here we find no suggestion of any such struggle. Darkness, in this passage — except in one or two creative translations — is not described as opposing the light. It is simply ignorant of the light's existence.

Moreover, the darkness here spoken of is not mindless. It possesses consciousness, otherwise the question of its comprehension or acceptance would not arise. Being darkness, however, it is incapable of "comprehending" the subtler reality of divine light.

St. John's reference here is not to Satan, but to the state of spiritual ignorance toward which Satan — an actual, universal force — ever seeks to draw souls. St. John is referring, rather, to the state of darkness, of ignorance itself. And he is suggesting that in man's unenlightened state of spiritual delusion, it is not possible to perceive, or "comprehend," the divine light.

To approach that light, then, we must rise above our ordinary human level of consciousness, and learn to live at that level in ourselves where God's light ever shines.

God's creation exists simultaneously on many different levels of manifestation. Even from science we know that there are realities far too subtle for us to perceive with our physical senses. The divine light — a reality beyond the perception of any physical science — forever surrounds us also. It cannot be overwhelmed or diminished by gross material realities, nor even related meaningfully to them on their own level of cosmic manifestation. For it occupies another level altogether.

By light, here, the Bible means the light of God, which is conscious. Thus, we may understand also that divine love is not understood, nor even touched, by human hatred. Divine joy is eternally above all human sorrow. Wisdom cannot be imagined, nor can it in any way be lessened, by ignorance. The way out of hatred, sorrow, and ignorance is by communion with God's inner light in our souls.

Ours is the choice. So long as we choose to live on a materialistic plane, we shall never behold the one true Light. So long as we choose to live selfishly, we shall never know divine love, for divine love is too lofty a reality to be comprehended on an ego level. So long as we choose those aggressive actions whose end is always suffering, we shall never know divine joy.

And yet, God's joy forever surrounds us. It dwells within us. It calls to us with longing in the silence of our souls, whispering eternally: "Reach out to Me. Claim Me for thy own!"

The ever-blissful Lord is never indifferent to our human griefs. His grace, however, awaits us on its own plane of reality. To know it, we, for our part, must reach up to it with devotion, in the deep silence of inner communion.

The darkness in us cannot comprehend the divine light. We must transcend our own inner darkness, if we would know the one true Light, which is God.

Thus it is, through the Holy Bible, that God has spoken to mankind.

Bhagavad Gita

God's Light Alone Is Real

This passage is from the eleventh Chapter, the 12th Stanza:

"If there should rise suddenly within the skies
Sunburst of a thousand suns
Flooding earth with beams undeemed–of,
Then might be that Holy One's
Majesty and radiance dreamed of!"

Commentary

The Bhagavad Gita here endeavors in words to express the inexpressible: the vision of God as Cosmic Light, as Cosmic Consciousness. Infinitely brighter God's light is than the light of countless suns crushed into one. Infinitely more majestic, more powerful is the Lord than the greatest majesty on earth; than the greatest power imaginable to man.

Unenlightened humanity, closing its eyes to higher truths, sees only darkness, and not the indwelling divine light. A small-minded person, confronted by greatness in anyone, judges what he sees according to his own pettiness. God, similarly, is imagined by many religionists as a sort of larger-than-life human being, possessing a man-like body, and subject to anger, jealousy, and similar human emotions.

Who indeed, can even imagine a conscious Being so great as to have brought into existence this vast universe, with its countless billions of stars and galaxies? Add to such a power the seemingly contradictory, because softening, quality of love, and describe that love as caring, separately and individually, for every creature in existence, and we have a concept that, for human beings, cannot even be clearly conceptualized.

God, the Scriptures say, is infinitely beyond mere human imagining. Those great saints who have communed with Him declare that only in such inner communion can the devotee find complete conviction, and eternal satisfaction.

As Paramhansa Yogananda wrote in *Autobiography of a Yogi*, the vision of God is "beyond imagination of expectancy." That cosmic consciousness, he said, is the only goal on earth worth striving for. It is an infinite love, which embraces every creature; a bliss ineffable, which calls to each of us to reclaim our eternal birthright in the Lord. Ultimately, there exists no other reality.

Thus, eternally, God has spoken to mankind.

Jesus: Window Onto the Infinite

Bible

The Infinite Christ

This passage is from the Gospel of St. John, Chapter 1, the 6th to the 14th Verses:

"There was a man sent from God, whose name was John. The same came for a witness, to bear witness of the Light, that all men through him might believe. He was not that Light, but was sent to bear witness of that Light. That was the true Light, which lighteth every man that cometh into the world. He was in the world, and the world was made by him, and the world knew him not. He came unto his own, and his own received him not. But as many as received him, to them gave he power to become the sons of God, even to them that believe on his name: Which were born, not of blood, nor of the will of the flesh, nor of the will of man, but of God. And the Word was made flesh,

and dwelt among us, (and we beheld his glory, the glory as of the only begotten of the Father,) full of grace and truth."

Commentary

The distinction drawn here by the Bible between John the Baptist and Jesus is important. John had attained to a high degree of spiritual advancement, one which enabled him to commune easily with the inner light. He could therefore "bear witness of it"; in other words, speak of it with authority. He had not yet, however, merged his consciousness in the Light so perfectly that he no longer saw himself as having a separate existence from that Light.

Jesus had attained such spiritual perfection. His ego had become dissolved in the Infinite. By God's grace, his consciousness was now united to the infinite Light. He was the Christ, the anointed of God. He and the Father were One.

We find here also another important distinction. The human mind is naturally drawn to Jesus in his humanity. St. John, however, even while speaking of him as living in a human body, describes him here in purely spiritual terms. "That," he says, "which lighteth every man that cometh into the world was the true light." He meant that Jesus "lighteth every man"; that Jesus "was the true light." Jesus, seen in this context, wasn't even what people saw as the man, Jesus: He was the infinite Christ. St. John doesn't even name him in this passage, though he names John the Baptist.

"He was in the world," says the Bible, "and the

world was made by him, and the world knew him not." The world, of course, knew the man, Jesus. St. John is telling us that Jesus was not the human being that he seemed to be. He was the Infinite Spirit — that which created the very universe. "The world was made by him," wrote St. John. It was this indwelling reality that the world knew not. They saw the outward human form, but that which they beheld with their physical eyes was only a channel for the higher reality.

It was people's mistaken perception of Jesus that prompted him to say to them elsewhere, "Before Abraham was, I am."

"He came unto his own," St. John tells us, "and his own received him not." The Jewish people, as a nation, were "his own," for they had chosen God. As Yogananda put it, "God chooses those who choose Him." Because of the Jews' conscious choice, the Lord in turn "chose" them.

The Jews as a people, however, little understood Whom it was, in reality, they had chosen. The majority could touch God only as if at the hem of His garment, through their human belief. Few, naturally, were advanced enough spiritually to know Him by direct inner perception.

Many times in the history of religion has God come to earth through His enlightened sons, in answer to the loving call of His devotees. Few, however, even among these — "His own" — are spiritually advanced enough to see beyond the outward, human form of the master to the indwelling Spirit.

All those who truly love Jesus should strive earnestly to probe beneath the surface of appearances

— beneath his outward humanity — beneath his beautiful earthly life — and discover the infinite Christ within. For that one Christ consciousness dwells forever in each of us.

Thus, through the Holy Bible, God has spoken to mankind.

Bhagavad Gita

The Meaning of Divine Incarnation

This passage is from the fourth Chapter, the 6th
and 7th Stanzas:

> *"Unborn, changeless, Lord of Creation and
> controller of My cosmic nature though I am, yet
> entering Nature I am dressed in the cosmic gar-
> ment of My own maya (delusion).*
> *"O Bharata, whenever virtue declines and vice
> predominates, I incarnate on earth. Taking visible
> form, I come to destroy evil and re-establish vir-
> tue."*

Commentary

Here the Bhagavad Gita confronts a great
mystery. God is described in both the Hindu and
Christian religions as having incarnated on earth: In

the Christian religion, as Jesus; in the Hindu, as Krishna and as other great masters who from time to time have been sent to earth as saviors of mankind.

Among orthodox Christians, there is no question of any other divine incarnation than that of Jesus. His birth is accepted as unique. The great mystery, therefore, of how such an event could have taken place is not deeply pondered. It is accepted as, quite simply, miraculous.

In the Hindu religion, however, because of the Scriptural promise of repeated incarnations of God, it is more natural that there should have been attempts made to explain the meaning of divine incarnation.

The vast Spirit, to begin with, would seem indeed to be conscious of mankind. Prayers have often been answered, many of them miraculously. Indeed, the concept of omnipresence implies infinitesimal smallness quite as much as infinite immensity. The same is true of the concept of omniscience. As Jesus put it, "The very hairs on your head are all numbered." (Matthew 10:30)

God has appeared in vision to saints in every age. He has been seen as a Light, heard as a Sound of many waters or of mighty thunder, felt as an overwhelming Love, or as infinite Bliss. His light has taken on form, human or otherwise. (To Moses He spoke out of a burning bush.) His sound has become a voice and expressed itself in human speech. His love has been manifested in the radiant gaze of the Divine Mother, or of Jesus, or Krishna, and in many other divine manifestations of light and ecstatic consciousness. No such experience could ever define

Him, in the sense of limiting Him. Yet every experience has manifested something of His infinite nature.

God created everything. Everything, therefore, in a sense, is His manifestation. In superconscious experiences, however, His manifestation is special, for it does not conceal the indwelling Spirit: It reveals it.

Divine visions express God's will openly to man. They spiritualize whomsoever they touch. They are a conscious revelation of the divine reality, in a way that material objects and unenlightened human beings can never be.

God's superconscious manifestations, in visions and the like, are always fleeting — like the waves on a sea. As the waves, in their movement and diversity, recall us ever to the sea's vastness, so divine manifestations are intended to recall our minds to the vast Reality they express.

There is nothing strange in the thought of God manifesting Himself in human form. He does so, indeed, in a sense every time He appears in vision to a saint. For through that saint's testimony, and through the magnetic influence of his ecstasy, the Lord becomes more of a vivid reality to others. God may be said to manifest Himself through every saint who lives in a state of inner communion with Him.

Such a saint, then, who is born in a state of constant communion because freed of the delusion of ego, may be said to be already, in a sense, an incarnation of the divine consciousness. If nothing remains of his limited ego, and if that master's consciousness is only of God's presence within, his very mission on earth is like a wave rising in full consciousness upon the surface of the infinite sea, expressing consciously — not itself — but the vast sea around it.

No wave could ever express that vastness perfectly. Nor could any divine manifestation in human form be God's only, unique, human manifestation.

God could no doubt manifest Himself on earth directly. He could even materialize a human body and live forever among men, thereby giving people everywhere a living focus for their devotion. Were He to do so, however, He would distract people from seeking Him in themselves, where alone He can actually be realized, and from expanding their little consciousness into His infinite bliss.

Jesus reminded his disciples, "The kingdom of God is within." The highest Scriptural teachings are ever a reminder of this truth: namely, that God must be sought within man, not outside of him through the senses.

No man is God. The wave cannot pretend to be the ocean. The ocean of divine awareness, however, which has become all the waves of physical phenomena, may be said to express itself consciously through those great souls whose consciousness is merged in the Lord.

We, too, as devotees, should strive always to "incarnate" the divine consciousness in our own lives. Let us live more by inner guidance. Let us strive to be channels of divine inspiration. Let us heed God's call in the soul to seek Him, to know Him, to merge in Him. Thus may we find release from our age-old delusion of separateness from His infinite bliss.

Thus, through the Bhagavad Gita, the Lord has spoken to mankind.

Week 5

The Son: Only Begotten, Because Omnipresent

Bible

The Christ Consciousness

This passage is from the Gospel of St. John, Chapter 1, the 14th Verse:

"And the Word was made flesh, and dwelt among us, (and we beheld his glory, the glory as of the only begotten of the Father,) full of grace and truth."

Commentary

This expression, "the only begotten of the Father," has a vast metaphysical significance. It refers not to the man, Jesus, but to his divine nature: to the infinite Christ consciousness of which Jesus was a human manifestation.

It is natural for human beings, seeing reality as we do with human eyes, to identify those statements in the Bible which refer to Jesus as divine with what we know of him as a man. This whole first part of St. John's Gospel, however, is so impersonal that it doesn't even name Jesus, although naming John the Baptist. St. John identifies Jesus as the infinite Light of God, the Word — "that which lighteth every man that cometh into the world."

Jesus, too, tried constantly to get people to see him not in his human, but in his divine aspect. As he put it in Matthew 18:20, "For where two or three are gathered together in my name, there am I in the midst of them." Had he identified himself with his human body, he could not have promised to be simultaneously present in all of the thousands of churches where people gathered together "in his name."

We often forget that Christ was not Jesus' name, but a title. It meant *the anointed*, and was used to refer to the Messiah, or Savior, of the Jews. Jesus referred to himself, similarly, as "him, whom the Father hath sanctified." (John 10:36)

This expression, then, "The only begotten of the Father," has a deep mystical significance, and is not intended to mean that Jesus, because born of the Holy Spirit and not by the agency of a human father, was literally the only offspring of God.

It should be kept in mind that other Saviors also — Buddha, for example — are believed by their followers to have been divinely born, without human paternal agency.

On the other hand, given the known immensity of God's creation, it is becoming increasingly difficult to imagine a unique divine manifestation. Modern astronomy has revealed a universe incredibly vast. In our galaxy alone there are estimated to be hundreds of billions of stars; in the whole universe, hundreds of billions of galaxies!

Science has found that the universe is also unimaginably ancient, extending backwards in time billions of years.

On our little planet Earth, the ruins of many ancient civilizations have been found. The history of this planet cannot in any way be limited to a steady progression of events over the brief space of a few centuries, at that tiny speck on our globe where the events of the Bible are known to have taken place.

It is difficult nowadays, if not impossible, to believe in the miraculous birth of just one "only begotten son," out of all the vast universe, on this one tiny planet, our earth.

Jesus himself tried constantly to get people to see in him *their own* highest potential. In John 14:12 he said, "Verily, verily, I say unto you, He that believeth in me, the works that I do shall he do also; and greater works than these shall he do; because I go unto my Father." And when the Jews, accusing him of blasphemy, said, "Thou, being a man, makest thyself God," he answered them, "Is it not written in your law, I said, *Ye* are gods?" (John 10:33,34)

This expression, "the only begotten of the Father," refers to the infinite Christ consciousness with which Jesus, "anointed" by God, was identified. The Christ consciousness is the "only begotten" because it is omnipresent. It is the divine reality which dwells at the heart of every atom of creation.

God the Father, the Creator, is beyond His creation. The Word, mentioned in the first sentence of St. John's Gospel, is that manifestation — that infinite vibration — proceeding out of the Father by which, as the Bible tells us, "all things were made." The Christ consciousness is the reflected presence of God in all creation.

Jesus was one with that infinite reality. This, then, is what the Bible means when it speaks of him as the "only begotten."

Thus, through the Holy Bible, God has spoken to mankind.

Bhagavad Gita

What Is an Avatar?

This passage is from the fourth Chapter, the 6th and 7th Stanzas:

> *"Unborn, changeless, Lord of Creation and controller of My cosmic nature though I am, yet entering Nature I am dressed in the cosmic garment of My own maya, or delusion.*
>
> *"O Bharata, whenever virtue declines and vice predominates, I incarnate on earth. Taking visible form, I come to destroy evil and re-establish virtue."*

Commentary

God may be said to incarnate, in a sense, through any great soul who, while living on earth, abides solely in His consciousness. The degree of His manifestation would depend on the depth of that saint's spiritual realization. Certainly, there would have to be some measure of direct inner perception, as opposed to living merely in the constant thought of God: some revelation on God's part of His ecstatic presence within.

In India, the concept of divine incarnation is traditionally applied not so much to those who in this life succeed in realizing God as to those masters who have been born with that realization. Many in India, therefore, believe that an incarnation of God must be a special creation of the Lord's, manifested uniquely by Him to dwell among men for a time in order to grant salvation to all who believe in Him.

Paramhansa Yogananda, however, explained the nature of a divine incarnation, rather, not as a special creation of God's, but as the return to earth of a soul that previously strove to find God, and became emancipated in Him. We find a hint of this same explanation in the Book of Revelation, where Jesus is quoted as saying, "To him that overcometh will I grant to sit with me in my throne, *even as I also overcame*, and am set down with my Father in his throne" (Revelation 3:21). Jesus' reference is clearly to his own overcoming, with the hope extended to all men that they, too, may overcome, and find freedom in God.

That is why Jesus said also (Matthew 5:46), "Be ye therefore perfect, even as your Father which is in heaven is perfect." To be as perfect as God can only mean to attain oneness with Him, as Jesus himself had attained.

A special creation of God's would be less in a

position to give people faith in their own spiritual capabilities. People need an example with which they can identify personally. That is the whole point of a divine incarnation. Much of the benefit of such an incarnation would be lost if God had to create a perfect human being simply because no actual human being could ever be found to fit the role. The obvious way, surely, to guide and inspire humanity would be to work through some qualified member of the human race: one who could inspire others with faith in their own potential for achievement.

For a person to grow in virtue, it is necessary for him to feel inspired from within. If he depends too heavily for his salvation on some outward channel, no matter how divine that channel, he will never develop the inner strength of character required for progress in the spiritual life. Rather, he may find, instead, just the excuse that human nature always seeks to persist in its human weaknesses. He may even condemn as presumptuous any effort on the part of others to grow in sanctity.

Spiritual progress is not for cowards and weaklings. It requires great inner strength. That is why the Bible, in John 1:12, says, "But as many as received him, to them gave he *power* to become the sons of God." The good news is that power is given to those who tune in humbly to the infinite, divine source. But it is given *from within*, and is always commensurate to man's own receptivity.

Paramhansa Yogananda explained the stages of spiritual development thus: A master who has so merged his consciousness in God as to be always awake in Him, having shed all vestiges of personal ego, is known as a *jivan mukta*: one "freed while living." Such a saint lives outwardly as a normal human being, but he is no longer limited, spiritually. Forever freed from earthly desires, his only reality is the infinite Lord.

Such a soul, however, at first still carries the vestigial memories of his past deeds, committed when he was still wedded to ego-consciousness. These memories, too, must be spiritualized gradually, their karmic threads unraveled, the mental image of each of them transformed into divine awareness.

God's presence must be realized in even the most worldly memories. For although the ego sees itself as separate from God, God is in truth everywhere. The most criminal behavior merely casts a veil — albeit a thick one! — over the indwelling divine reality. The enlightened master, freed from the bondage of delusion, must align also his old self with that present realization.

Once freedom is attained from past actions as well — a state rarely achieved on this material level of existence — the soul becomes a *param mukta*, or fully liberated soul.

When such a soul is reborn on earth, he comes as a full divine incarnation, or *purna avatar*. God's power radiates through him in a way that it cannot through any lesser being, however enlightened. Even a fully liberated master, a *param mukta*, can uplift into the divine light only a limited number of disciples. But a divine incarnation can draw to God as many as come to him for help.

Thus, through the Bhagavad Gita, God has spoken to mankind.

How To Attain the Highest Wisdom

Bible

The Importance of Soul-Receptivity

This passage is from the Gospel of St. John, Chapter 1, Verse 12:

"But as many as received him, to them gave he power to become the sons of God, even to them that believe on his name."

Commentary

Spiritual teaching is of many different kinds:
Moral maxims offer general admonitions for the proper conduct of human affairs. Readings from the Scriptures give moral maxims the authoritative stamp of divine law. Stories and sayings from the lives of saints provide devotional guidelines for those who aspire to live godly lives. Wise, personal counseling supplies essential guidance — more so,

generally, than anything one merely reads.

Among these outward ways of teaching, living examples of the spiritual life are the most effective of all.

None of this teaching, however, can change us to the same extent as transformation that is effected from within ourselves. In every field of endeavor, outward teaching, though always necessary, withholds this most vital of all keys to success.

Many students go to art school to learn how to paint. There they learn useful rules and techniques. But how many of them actually go on after school to become great artists?

Many students of science are taught all the known laws of physics. Still, how many go on to become great physicists?

Business principles, similarly, are studied by thousands. Yet how many students, on the strength of that knowledge alone, develop into successful businessmen?

Many, indeed, who do become great artists, scientists, and businessmen, during their school years were not even particularly good students. What made them outstanding in their fields later on was some spark each of them had in himself: some insight, some quality of energy, some sort of subtle magnetism.

Were it possible to transmit such a spark to others, instead of merely passing on theoretical information, it might be possible also to ensure the graduation of geniuses from our universities. No one so far, unfortunately — at least in the field of human endeavor — has found a way to transmit such a spark. Indeed, it wouldn't suffice even to know how to offer it: The student also would need to know how to "receive" it.

In this passage of St. John's Gospel, we read that there is one field of endeavor — the spiritual — in which this special spark, this inner power, can be transmitted. The power referred to is that of divine grace. On man's part, what is needed primarily is the faith and devotion — the true willingness — to receive it without reservation into the deepest reaches of his inner being.

Such direct transfer to the soul, rather than any indirect approach through the intellect or the emotions, is by far the most effective way of transmitting spiritual understanding. Any other form of teaching is, by its very nature, hearsay. Divine grace alone can lift the devotee above the treadmill of human endeavor, and give him the dynamic energy he needs to soar towards God.

God works through channels. His grace comes to man primarily through those great souls in whom its presence is already revealed.

God gives His love equally to all. Those who seek Him with devotion will be led progressively through books and lesser teachers to one, finally, who will be for him a direct, personal channel of God's grace. As the devotee learns to be receptive to whatever channels God sends him, he develops finally the purity of heart to attract to himself the fully open channel of one who himself knows God. Becoming ever more deeply attuned to this divine channel, he attains levels of divine awareness that are simply not attainable by the power of human thought alone — levels of insight that are unreachable by even the most positive resolutions of the human will.

The Bible says that this power was transmitted "even to them who believe on his name." Deep soul-receptivity, of course, goes far beyond merely "believing on his name," and attracts a far greater outpouring of grace. Even relatively superficial receptivity, however, can bestow true spiritual benefits. As a person's name may suffice to recall the person himself to our minds, so even the name of Jesus, or that of any other great master, when repeated with devotion, can focus our attention on him as a channel of God's grace, and thereby help us to attune ourselves to the divine consciousness in which he himself inwardly lives.

It helps, therefore, to sing the name of Jesus, as well as that of other great masters: to call to them repeatedly — not in a spirit of idolatry, but with love for the Lord whose grace they channel to us — love for the infinite light and love in which we ourselves seek to merge.

What Jesus accomplished, each of us, too, must accomplish. We also, as this passage of the Bible affirms, have the hope, the promise — indeed, the high spiritual duty to "become the sons of God."

Thus, through the Holy Bible, God has spoken to mankind.

Bhagavad Gita

Inviting the Light

This passage is from the tenth Chapter, the 10th and 11th Stanzas:

> *"To those who are ever attached to Me, and who worship Me with love, I impart discernment, by means of which they attain Me.*
> *"Out of My love for them, I, the Divine within them, set alight in them the radiant lamp of wisdom, thereby dispelling the darkness of their ignorance."*

Commentary

Here, the Bhagavad Gita speaks, as this week's passage from the Bible did, of the importance of divine grace in the search for God.

Human striving alone can never lift the spiritual

aspirant into divine realms. Many students of yoga make the mistake of thinking that by their will power alone, exerted through the daily practice of breathing exercises, physical postures, and meditation techniques, they will attain cosmic consciousness. Their approach to the spiritual life is almost as if God were a sort of divine mountain, to be conquered in a spirit of mountaineering bravado! That is hardly the spirit in which to approach yoga, that highest of spiritual sciences!

Such misguided aspirants fail to realize that the secret of effective yoga practice, like that of any true spiritual practice, is deep love. Plumbing the depths of ego, rather than those of the soul, they separate themselves from their fellowman in an attitude of spiritual aloofness, and end up drowning in the delusion of pride.

The essence of spiritual development, always, is steadily increasing receptivity to God's light and grace, through deep, humble love for the Lord. The goal of yoga practice, then, is simply this: to deepen one's receptivity by stilling the body, mind, and emotions, thereby making oneself more sensitively aware of the movement of divine grace within.

As spiritual aspirants, we must open ourselves to *receive* God in ourselves. The Bhagavad Gita shows us the way. That spiritual aspirant can "receive" God truly in himself who practices attachment to Him, instead of to the world; who lovingly worships Him, as a means of driving out of the heart all worldly infatuation; who holds fast to an attitude of mental openness and humility, in which soil alone discriminative wisdom, or discernment, can flourish; who invites God's light into the darkest corners of his being; and who, above all, surrenders to the infinite Love.

In God's love for us, and in the power of loving which that love awakens in us, we can receive the grace by which alone our souls can know God.

Thus, through the Bhagavad Gita, God has spoken to mankind.

God Is Above the Law

Bible

The Law Is Perfected in Love

This passage is from the Gospel of St. John, Chapter 1, Verse 17:

"The law was given by Moses, but grace and truth came by Jesus Christ."

Commentary

At the time when God gave the law to Moses, the need was for the tribes of Israel, recently liberated from four centuries of slavery in Egypt, to be molded into a single, homogeneous nation. Basically, the Ten Commandments, as well as the six hundred other, lesser, laws, were moral guidelines for a God-fearing people. It was as if God had said to them through Moses, "You have chosen, as a nation, to live according to My ways. I now give you rules by which you as a nation can be pleasing to

Me."

Some of the Ten Commandments can be interpreted mystically as well. For example, the deeper meaning of, "Thou shalt have no other gods before me," is, "Direct all your desires and devotion toward Me alone" — an offering possible only in deep inner communion with the Lord. God's intention, however, was clearly the religious discipline of a whole people — only a few of whom could have been mystically inclined.

In the normal course of spiritual evolution, outward religious observances precede inward, mystical aspiration. Man must learn first to fear God, and obey Him. Only gradually, as he learns to live for God, does he come to love Him.

The Jews, having dedicated themselves in faith to the Lord, initiated their spiritual development as a people. Their first step, following this divine choice, was to purify themselves, by observing the set of disciplinary rules that Moses gave them. Gradually, by observance of the law, they refined their attunement to God's will.

Jesus Christ was sent to earth by God when there were sufficient numbers ready for the next step on the journey to attract a new dispensation. It was the spiritual hunger of the Jewish people that attracted this divine response. Jesus was sent to instruct his countrymen in the ways of love.

Referring to the spiritual unpreparedness of the Jews of Moses' times, Jesus himself once told his orthodox critics (Mark 10:5), "For the hardness of your heart [Moses] wrote this precept."

Jesus came also to teach the Jewish people the

true meaning of liberation — that is to say, freedom not from outward slavery, such as they had known in Egypt, but from the inward bondage of delusion, from material desires and attachments, and from the arrogant demands of a self-affirming ego.

Out of the myriad prayers of Judaism, Jesus gave as his first commandment this one: "Thou shalt love the Lord thy God with all thy heart, and with all thy soul, and with all thy mind, and with all thy strength." (Mark 12:30) His second commandment was "like unto it": "Thou shalt love thy neighbor as thyself."

It was not Jesus' intention to break away from Jewish tradition. As he said in Matthew 5:17, "Think not that I am come to destroy the law, or the prophets: I am not come to destroy, but to fulfill." It was his stated purpose not to found a new religion, but to add to the old one this refinement of love, and, through love, of living consciously in God's grace.

Love, according to divine law itself, is above any law. Jesus' teaching was not to those whose devotion was centered in the law. It was to those who were spiritually awakened enough to want a personal relationship with God, as their divine Father.

The evolutionary development from Judaism to what ended up becoming Christianity has continued to the present day. The emphasis of Christians on a more personal relationship with God has developed over centuries into a hunger not only for outward, but for inward, direct communion with the Lord.

Thus it occurred by God's grace in our time that Paramhansa Yogananda was sent to the West, to teach the secrets of meditation and inner communion.

Those who recognize the inescapability of divine law should seek always to live by it. Those, again, who have learned to live by the law should seek its fulfillment in divine grace, love, and wisdom.

And those, finally, who believe deeply in God's grace should seek to receive it in themselves as a conscious experience. If they believe deeply in His love, they should seek direct communion with that love, in prayer and meditation. And if they believe in His truth and wisdom, they should seek themselves always to grow in wisdom and divine perception.

For thus, through the Holy Bible, God has spoken to mankind.

Bhagavad Gita

Divine Love: The End of All Observances

This passage is from the eighteenth Chapter, the
64th to the 66th Stanzas:

> "Nay! but once more
> Take My last word, My utmost meaning
>   have!
> Precious thou art to Me; right well beloved!
> Listen! I tell thee for thy comfort this.
> Give Me thy heart! adore Me! serve Me! cling
> In faith and love and reverence to Me!
> So shalt thou come to Me! I promise true,
> For thou art sweet to Me!
>   "And let go those —
> Rites and writ duties! Fly to me alone!
> Make Me thy single refuge! I will free
> Thy soul from all its sins! Be of good cheer!"

Commentary

Here Krishna speaks to Arjuna of a path higher than that of formal religious observances; higher than that of fasting, rituals, good deeds, and charitable offerings. The path referred to is that of one-pointed devotion to the Lord.

In no way is Krishna belittling those spiritual aspirants who strive valiantly to adhere to the commandments of the law. A path, however, should not be confused with its goal.

The ultimate goal of all religion is union with God. The commandments of Scripture provide rules of behavior for people in various walks of life, simply that they may grow from ego-attachment toward final awakening in the Lord.

By abiding by such a commandment as harmlessness ("Thou shalt not kill," in the Mosaic law), one comes gradually to feel his oneness with all life.

By following the commandment of non-covetousness ("Thou shalt not steal," and, "Thou shalt not covet," in the Mosaic law), one gradually reaches a state of centeredness, of rest in himself. From such inward peace springs the inclination to probe the inner, spiritual depths.

By adhering to truthfulness ("Thou shalt not bear false witness," in Moses' law), one develops the discernment to penetrate through clouds of delusion, and to understand the deeper nature of things.

No one would advise a child to bypass arithmetic and pass straight on to the study of higher mathematics. Nevertheless, once he masters higher mathematics he may lose some of his familiarity with the simple rules of arithmetic.

There is a story of the two famous scientists, Einstein and Eddington. They were discussing some abstruse point of physics, when they hit an arithmetical snag. Finding themselves in difficulty, they called in an accountant to help them!

On the spiritual path as well, elaborate attention to the intricacies of outward rule and ritual is an aid only for beginners. It serves to keep their minds engaged in God-reminding activities, and thereby diverted from ego-active pursuits.

Too much fussy attention to detail, however, becomes a distraction, as one develops the ability to live ever more constantly by inner, divine inspiration.

To one living in ecstatic inner communion with God, the lesser rules of spirituality — the deeper purpose of which is only to guide devotees toward such communion — may be a hindrance instead of a help. It isn't that at this high spiritual level one can steal, lie, and harm people with impunity. Rather, the more centered one is in God, the more his actions are in natural harmony with God's law. He needs no special instructions or formal observances to guide him toward mental alignment with that law.

The important thing to understand here is that there is a higher purpose to religious observances. The commandments are not rules to follow merely to please God. Rather, they were given to man to help refine human nature, thereby to make it a fit vehicle for the manifestation of soul-consciousness. Outward observances are meant to develop, and not to obstruct, the ability to love God and to live in true, heart-felt charity toward one's neighbor.

That is why Jesus said, "The sabbath was made for man, and not man for the sabbath." (Mark 2:27) The souls he had come to help were ready for this higher teaching of divine love and charity. Some of them, indeed, were ready also for the highest teaching — that of inner communion, directed toward ultimate union with the Lord. To these true disciples he spoke individually, and in depth. Others he taught in parables, only hinting at higher teachings with the oft-repeated words, "He that hath ears to hear, let him hear."

Sri Krishna also followed the above passage in the Bhagavad Gita with a warning not to share this highest teaching — the call to divine love as the straightest path to God — except with those devotees who would truly understand it, and would not use it as an excuse to ignore the commandments of God's law.

Moses taught primarily through the law. Yet Moses, too, was a true master. The higher teachings can be seen — as it were, hidden — in his life, and in the law he gave.

Jesus taught the higher divine truths more openly, because in his day people were more generally ready to receive them.

In our age, Paramhansa Yogananda no longer needed to have recourse to parables and veiled statements. His great contribution to the history of religion, made possible by people's increased hunger for spiritual understanding, was to present long-hidden truths so simply that virtually anyone could accept them, and understand clearly — if only with their intellects — to what end the spiritual path is directed.

Thus, through the Bhagavad Gita, God has spoken to mankind.

How To See God

Bible

The Triune Nature of God

This passage is from the Gospel of St. John, Chapter 1, Verse 18:

"No man hath seen God at any time; the only begotten Son, which is in the bosom of the Father, he hath declared him."

Commentary

The first reference here means, "No *human being* has ever seen God." In the statement, "He hath declared him," the meaning is, "He has given us knowledge of him."

No human being — no one, that is to say, with only the vision possible to physical eyes — can see God, for the divine realms are too subtle for merely human perception. St. John did not mean, however, that it is impossible for man to rise above his physical senses and to see God with the eyes of the soul.

Jesus said, in the Beatitudes, "Blessed are the pure in heart: *for they shall see God.*"

Again, (in Luke 17:20, 21) he said, "The kingdom of God cometh not with observation: Neither shall they say, Lo here! or, lo there! for behold, the kingdom of God is within you."

Jesus said also (in John 14:7), "If ye had known me, ye should have known my Father also: and from henceforth ye know him, *and have seen him.*"

"Go within," Jesus was saying in effect. "*In your souls* you shall see God."

St. John tells us, as we find Jesus doing repeatedly, to seek God in inner communion, and not only in outward religious observances. In the sense intended by St. John in this passage, it wasn't Jesus, the man, who gave us knowledge of the Father. For St. John speaks of him as the "Son which is in the bosom of the Father" — that is to say, as the infinite, divine reality that dwelt consciously within Jesus.

John's reference is to the Christ consciousness: "that which lighteth every man that cometh into the world"; Him also of whom St. John said that the very world was made by Him.

That Christ consciousness, as we saw in an earlier reading, is described as "the only begotten Son," for the Christ consciousness — God's projected consciousness in creation — is infinite. There cannot be more than one such reflection.

God became the Word, or Holy Ghost. His Word, too, is divine. It *is* God. For the Word is God's consciousness in vibration. It is the mighty, vibratory Sound by which God gave outward expression to His creative spirit. Vibration was needed to produce the manifested universe. Without movement, the very atoms would resolve back once again into the Infinite. On this principle of movement rests the entire cosmos.

Movement, however, is not the essence of Spirit, which is forever calm and at rest in Itself. Vibratory creation is an appearance, merely: a dream in the mind of the Cosmic Dreamer. Behind every vibration, calmly sustaining it, is the still consciousness of the infinite Spirit. Because the Spirit resides outside of His creation, God's calm, unmoving consciousness at the heart of all vibratory creation is described as the Son: the "only begotten," because it's the universal projection of God's consciousness into creation.

We have thus the eternal Trinity: the Father, beyond creation: that unmoving Spirit by whom was dreamed into existence all that is; the Holy Ghost: the mighty vibration of God's Word, forever divinely conscious, out of which emanated the vibrating atoms of creation; and the Son: the reflected, calm consciousness of the Father reflected in, but forever undisturbed by, His vibratory creation.

That is what Jesus meant when he said (in John 14:6), "I am the way, the truth, and the life: no man cometh unto the Father, but by me." God's calm, unmoving presence must be realized first *in* His creation, for that is where our consciousness is now. Only then can it be realized in its pure essence, as the Spirit beyond creation.

This grand mystery is presented in the most ancient spiritual teachings: God in three aspects, yet forever One: God the Father, beyond creation; God the Son, in creation; and God the Holy Ghost — the vast Spirit *as* creation.

This explanation is found in very ancient revelation. It concerns the Trinity described also by great masters in ancient India, the Trinity which is known in those Scriptures as *Aum* (the Holy Ghost), *Tat* (the Kutastha Chaitanya, or Christ consciousness), and *Sat*, the Spirit beyond creation.

Thus, then, through the Holy Bible, God has spoken to mankind.

Bhagavad Gita

Visualizing Infinity

This passage is from the eleventh Chapter, the 8th Stanza:

> *"'Thou canst not see Me with mortal eyes. Therefore I now give thee sight divine. Behold My supreme power of Yoga!'*
>
> *"With these words Hari, the exalted Lord of Yoga, revealed himself to Arjuna in His infinite form."*

Commentary

The meaning of *hari* is "thief." Here, it applies to God as the "Thief of hearts." For God's love, once felt in the heart, is so attractive that it steals away our love from every lesser object of affection. His love is great enough to overwhelm every human

77

desire. He is described in the Scriptures as *rasa*: supremely relishable.

As St. Jean Vianney, a Christian mystic, said, "If only you knew how much God loves you, you would die for joy!"

Sri Krishna makes it clear in this passage that we cannot see God with merely human vision. Nor can we behold Him by our human will alone. Our devotional desire to behold Him must be strong, but we must nevertheless understand that it is by God's grace alone that we can gain entry into highest spiritual realms.

God's reality is far beyond human power to conceptualize. For human understanding it is unimaginably vast, inconceivably impersonal, incomprehensibly abstract: an infinite Light; a Sound (as of many waters); an overwhelming Love; an indescribable Bliss. Even to speak of God in human terms is misleading, for He has no form as we can understand the word.

If we would know Him, it is important to live in the thought of Infinity, and to eschew the petty realities of this world. If we strive always to live in divine consciousness, so the Scriptures have promised, we shall eventually win God's response.

The devotee should meditate every day on the Infinite Vastness.

Think of God, therefore, not only within the bounds of your imagination — as a Father, Mother, or divine Friend. But think of Him also as that Infinite Being out of which the vast universe was brought into existence; as that supernal Consciousness toward which all your highest inspirations aspire.

Meditate on an expanding Light:

Visualize it, first, as a shining point in the center of your forehead. Expand that light outward from between your eyebrows, and feel it flowing over your entire body, filling every cell of your body with light.

Jesus spoke of this light when he said (Matthew 6:22), "The light of the body is the eye: if therefore thine eye be single, thy whole body shall be full of light."

Visualize this light expanding beyond the boundaries of your body, to become an aura of golden light surrounding it. Think of this aureole, rather than of your physical form, as your true body.

Go on expanding the light. Fill the place where you are sitting with shimmering, golden light: the room, the building, your surrounding neighborhood. Expand the light further still. Behold it spanning the nations of the earth, the continents, the oceans — the whole world. From your heart, send rays of that light outward in blessing to all mankind.

At last, release your light from its earthly limitations. Behold it streaming outward joyously into all the solar system, into the vast galaxy. Behold it filling the entire universe.

Meditate daily in this way. Thus, your mind will become freed gradually to soar on wings of rising inspiration in God.

As the Holy Bible states (Isaiah 55:8,9), "My thoughts are not your thoughts, neither are your ways my ways, saith the Lord. For as the heavens are higher than the earth, so are my ways higher than your ways, and my thoughts than your thoughts."

And thus, through the Bhagavad Gita, God has spoken to mankind.

Part II

The Instruments of Recognition

How To Study the Scriptures

Bible

Use the Gifts God Has Given You!

This passage begins with the Gospel of St. Matthew, Chapter 15, Verses 1-20:

"Then some of the scribes and Pharisees from Jerusalem came and asked Jesus, 'Why do your disciples break our ancient tradition and eat their food without washing their hands properly first?'

"'Tell me,' replied Jesus, 'why do you break God's commandment through your tradition? For God said, "Honor thy father and thy mother," and, "He that speaketh evil of father and mother, let him die the death." But if a man tells his parents, "Whatever money I might have given you I now give to God (as a donation to the temple)," you say that [in this respect] he is absolved of the need to honor his father or his mother. And so your tradition empties the commandment of God of all its meaning. You hypocrites! Isaiah described you beautifully when he said:

"'"This people honoreth me with their lips;
But their heart is far from me. But in vain do they
worship me, teaching as their doctrines the precepts of men."'

"Then he called the crowd to him and said,
'Listen, and understand this thoroughly! It is not
what goes <u>into</u> a man's mouth that makes him
common or unclean. It is what comes <u>out</u> of a
man's mouth that makes him unclean.'

"Later his disciples came to him and said, 'Do
you know that the Pharisees are deeply offended by
what you said?'

"'Every plant which my Heavenly Father did
not plant will be pulled up by the roots,' returned
Jesus. 'Let them alone, They are blind guides, and
when one blind man leads another blind man they
will both end up in the ditch!'

"'Explain this parable to us,' broke in Peter.

"'Are you still unable to grasp things like
this?' replied Jesus. 'Don't you see that whatever
goes <u>into</u> the mouth passes into the stomach and
then out of the body altogether? But the things
that come <u>out</u> of a man's mouth come from his
heart and mind, and it is they that really make a
man unclean. For it is from a man's mind that
evil thoughts arise — murder, adultery, lust, theft,
perjury and blasphemy. These are the things
which make a man unclean, not eating without
washing his hands properly!'"

Commentary

Jesus' vigorous reply to the Pharisees was clearly

intended not primarily as a dissertation on parental respect, but rather on true, as opposed to outward and superficial, respect for the Scriptures. In passing only, therefore, may the comment be made that his statement on respect for one's parents can be understood as an insinuation that the Pharisees blessed people for donating to the temple, because such donations found their way into their own priestly pockets. This alone would explain Jesus' accusation that the Pharisees had substituted the precepts of men for the commandments of God.

For had the question really concerned only dedicating one's money to God rather than giving it to one's parents, there are enough Scriptural statements to the effect that God should come first in everything. Jesus himself consistently taught that God should come first in everything. Once, when told that his mother and brethren wanted to see him, he answered with the question: "Who is my mother, or my brethren?" Then he looked at those who were sitting around him, and said, "Behold my mother and my brethren! For whosoever shall do the will of God, the same is my brother, and my sister, and mother." (Mark 3:33-35)

The point of this quotation here, then, concerns the larger question of how rightly to understand the Scriptures. The episode quoted is an example of the constant opposition Jesus faced from the over-orthodox Pharisees — scholarly men of dogma-circumscribed understanding — who condemned him for the new interpretations he was placing on traditionally accepted readings of the Scriptures.

They kept trying to engage him in scriptural debate. But such discussion obviously held no interest for him. Rarely do we find him answering his Scripture-quoting critics with contrasting quotations of his own. And whenever he did quote the Scriptures, it was as we find him doing here: using common sense to show the orthodox where their human traditions had strayed from the original, true meaning of the Scriptures.

Otherwise, when he appealed to the Scriptures it was usually to claim, but in a general way, that they endorsed his teaching. Never do we find him descending to the level of Scriptural polemic, point by elaborate point, as the theological fundamentalists of his day were accustomed to doing, and as so many do who vigorously promote him in our own day.

"You search the scriptures," he said in John 5:39, "imagining that in them you will find eternal life. And all the time they give their testimony to me!"

The New Testament shows clearly that Jesus considered mere intellectual knowledge of the Scriptures far from adequate to true understanding. As we read (Luke 24:45): "Then he opened their minds, *so that they might understand the scriptures.*" Jesus, in other words, appealed not only to Scriptural authority, but above all to people's *ability to understand that authority.*

Again and again, moreover, we find him saying that, without love, no true understanding is possible. As he proclaimed to his critics, after speaking to them of their practice of searching the Scriptures, "But I know you, that ye have not the love of God in you."

He appealed also to men's natural spiritual sympathies. To those who challenged him, saying, "Is it lawful to heal on the sabbath day?" he replied (Matthew 12:11,12): "If any of you had a sheep which fell into a ditch on the Sabbath day, would he not take hold of it and pull it out? How much more valuable is a man than a sheep? Of course it is right to do good on the Sabbath day!"

And when he accepted the devoted ministrations of a woman, though sinful, he answered the unspoken criticism of his host, a self-righteous Pharisee, by saying, "Her sins, which are many, are forgiven; for she loved much: but to whom little is forgiven, the same loveth little." (Luke 7:47)

We too, then, when we study the Scriptures, should use the instruments of understanding that Jesus recommended. In prayer and meditation let us strive to penetrate behind the words and understand them with the intuition of our hearts. Let us base our perception in love for God, and in charity for our fellowman. Pure, divine love was the ultimate essence of Jesus' teaching.

And let us recognize also, in his constant appeal to common sense, an affirmation of one of the most valuable assets God has given to man. For dogmatism is the coward's defense against any challenge of the unfamiliar.

People who oppose any expansion of their awareness, and who justify their stand by an uncritical appeal to tradition, are the kind of believers to whom Jesus was referring when he said (Luke 5:36): "Nobody tears a piece from a new coat to patch up an old one. If he does, he ruins the new one and the new piece does not match the old." New, fresh insights into truth are better offered to fresh, open spirits, and not to those faded intellects whose mental fiber has been rubbed thin by constant contact with old habits. Such habit-bound believers Jesus did not even try to convince, repeating only, "He that hath ears to hear, let him hear."

Jesus' life and mission was a stirring appeal to the highest of all life's adventures: the search for God, and for divine truth. "Truth," as Paramhansa Yogananda put it, "is not afraid of questions." Jesus, by his constant teaching and example, challenged his listeners never to accept fixed ideas and definitions in place of the actual, direct experience of truth.

As he said to Nicodemus (John 3:11): "Verily, verily, I say unto thee, We speak that we do know, and testify that we have seen."

To perceive the truth directly with the purified eyes of the soul is the high summons of Christ's life. As he put it, "Ye shall know the truth, and the truth shall make you free." (John 8:32)

And thus, through the Holy Bible, God has spoken to mankind.

Bhagavad Gita

The Need for Single-Mindedness

This passage is from the second Chapter, the 41st Stanza:

"The intellects of those who lack fixity of spiritual purpose are inconstant, their interests endlessly ramified."

Commentary

True understanding, as the Bhagavad Gita frequently points out, is not possible without inner mental clarity. And mental clarity, as we learn here, cannot be achieved without one-pointed resolve.

People whose lives are not directed by high aspiration often become spiritual vagabonds. Some of them drift in desultory fashion from theory to theory, from teaching to teaching, and from teacher to

teacher. Others lose themselves in the endless laby-
rinth of theological discussion and debate. Never do
such persons achieve firm understanding, which is
born only of direct inner perception.

Many such people endlessly pursue new religious teachings, like children chasing after but-
terflies. But they remain forever discontented in
themselves.

This is one of the pitfalls on the spiritual path:
fickleness — the tendency to confuse novelty and the
fleeting enthusiasm it brings with the changeless joy
of divine awakening. People who lack deep spiritual commitment often mistake the babbling brook
of emotional release for the mighty river of divine
love. Faced, once their first burst of enthusiasm has
been spent, with the prospect of long, hard, daily
work on themselves, their dedication falters, and
their spirits sag. They become easily attracted to any
new teaching that seems to them to offer faster, and
especially easier, results.

"Outsiders come," Paramhansa Yogananda once
said, "and see only the surface. Sooner or later they
drift away. But those who are our own, they never
leave."

The masters devote their energies to those who
are, as Yogananda put it, "their own" — those, in
other words, who know deeply in their hearts that it
is God alone they want. Such souls are soon led by
God to that path which is right for them. Once finding their own true path, they never leave it.

There was a time in the life of Jesus when, as we
read in the 6th Chapter of the Gospel of St. John,

"Many of his disciples went back, and walked no more with him." To those who were close to him, Jesus said, "Will you also go away?" And Simon Peter answered, "Lord, to whom shall we go?"

There is a second kind of spiritual drifter: not the one who wanders endlessly from teaching to teaching, but one, rather, whose thoughts drift endlessly — from doubt to spiritual doubt, or from one intellectual explanation of Scripture to another. Such a person may think to find in endless ramifications of subtle definitions some final insight into reality. The truth, however, constantly eludes him.

Endlessly thinking, endlessly quoting, endlessly debating the fine points of Scripture — such mental vagrancy is for pedestrian minds. Sri Krishna, here in the Bhagavad Gita, urges us to fix our minds in one-pointed aspiration on the Lord. Only thus will our discrimination, like an arrow sped from a bow, fly straight into the heart of Infinity.

And thus, through the Bhagavad Gita, God has spoken to mankind.

Dogmatism vs. Common Sense

Bible

A Good Tree Brings Forth Good Fruits

This passage is from the Gospel of St. Matthew, Chapter 7, Verses 15-20:

> *"Beware of false prophets, which come to you in sheep's clothing, but inwardly they are ravening wolves. Ye shall know them by their fruits. Do men gather grapes of thorns, or figs of thistles? Even so every good tree bringeth forth good fruit; but a corrupt tree bringeth forth evil fruit.*
> *"A good tree cannot bring forth evil fruit, neither can a corrupt tree bring forth good fruit. Wherefore by their fruits ye shall know them."*

Commentary

Jesus here is pleading with his listeners to use their God-given common sense.

The way of bigotry is ever to silence reason by appealing to unquestioned authority. It is a curious phenomenon of human nature that fanatical insistence on any point always increases in direct proportion to a person's inability to prove his point! The greater the likelihood that a theory might be tested, the less voluble do its supporters become.

Such, essentially, is the contribution to religion on the part of modern science. It isn't that science is particularly concerned with religious issues, but rather that the scientific method has introduced a new approach to reality itself: that of testing one's beliefs, and never accepting any theory blindly.

Most people credit science with having invented this eminently reasonable approach. In this two-thousand-year-old statement, however, we find Jesus himself advocating it!

Nowhere, indeed, do we find him dogmatically indoctrinating his followers. It is true, he made extraordinary claims. So also would any of us seem to do, were we able to travel backwards in time and describe to people in the middle ages the wonders of radio, television, and space travel. Jesus had experienced the divine realms in all their infinite glory. How could he describe them believably to people whose experience of life was limited to the world as they knew it through their physical senses?

And yet, Jesus never counseled blind belief. In telling people, "This is what I have experienced, and what you also will experience if you follow me," he emphasized constantly the experience, not the theory, of his teaching: the fruits of spiritual living, and not merely the authoritarian commandment to live by the Scriptures and ask no questions.

To Nicodemus (John 3:11) he said, "Verily, verily, I say unto thee, We speak that which we do know, and testify that which we have seen." And again: "Art thou a master of Israel, and knowest not these things?" His obvious implication was that what he taught was something others might know also. Jesus, in other words, was not hoarding divine secrets, but was offering to share them with everyone who would receive them with understanding.

To the woman of Samaria (John 4:22) he said, "We *know* what we worship," adding, "But the hour cometh, and now is, when the true worshipers shall worship the Father in spirit and in truth: for the Father seeketh such to worship him."

And so we find that his way was not to answer dogma with dogma, but to plead with people, if they hadn't the intuition to recognize in their souls the truths he was teaching, at least to use their God-given common sense. "Judge a teaching by its fruits" was his classic response to bigotry.

And when the Pharisees accused him of being an instrument of Satan for casting devils out of people, he replied (Matthew 12:25,26): "Any kingdom divided against itself is bound to collapse. Nor can any household divided against itself last for long. If Satan were expelling Satan, he would be divided against himself. How, then, could his kingdom continue?" And again he added, "You can tell a tree at once by its fruit."

It should be noted, incidentally, in the passage first quoted above, that Jesus was not warning people against prophets generally, but only against false ones. Had his warning been directed at all future prophets, he would not have bothered to offer this test for a prophet's genuineness.

One common attribute of common sense is a sense of humor — the consequence of a refined sense of proportion, and the corresponding ability to see the one in relation to the many. Thus, the self-importance of a petty bureaucrat, for instance, is not accepted at his own evaluation, but rather is viewed with amusement.

The most evident sign of the fanatic, frequently, is his total lack of humor — the result of his lack of any sense of proportion. For the bigot, the most trivial article of his faith appears to demand valiant defense against the forces of hell itself — enough of a challenge to dull the laughter in any eye!

Tradition presents Jesus as "one who never was known to smile" — to quote the early Jewish historian, Josephus. Yet we find countless passages in the Gospels where it is difficult not to visualize him with at least a quietly humorous smile, if not actually laughing joyously.

Consider the delightful skill with which he answered the Pharisees' charge that he was an instrument of Satan!

Consider also his amusing word portrait (Matthew 6:2) of those hypocrites who, when bringing alms to the temple, hired trumpeters to precede them to make sure that everyone applauded their piety. Do we not imagine him smiling also as he added, "Verily, they have their reward!"?

Jesus offered his followers the supernal gift of divine joy — a joy, as he put it, "that no one will be able to take from you." (John 16:22) Does not joy itself find its most natural human expression in delighted laughter?

Let us remember, finally, the parable of the talents. In that story, a man returning from a long journey praised two of his servants who, by wise investment, had doubled the money he'd left in their keeping. Next, he fired a third servant who, instead of putting his share of the money to good use, had buried it "safely" in the ground.

A talent in those days was the name for a unit of money. From that name our own word, talent, is derived — possibly in recognition of this very story. For what Jesus was referring to was the natural gifts with which God has endowed His human children. And what he was saying was, "Use those gifts. Don't deny them in the ignorant belief that God will be pleased with you for accepting my words blindly. Don't suppress your native common sense, but use it, as well as your other God-given faculties, to help you to arrive at the truth. For what I have taught you must be able to stand up under every honest investigation, or else it is not true. Above all, never fear to subject what I teach you to the test of your own experience."

To God we should offer the very best that is in us. Above all, we should never fear to be completely honest with ourselves, and with Him, in our search for Him.

For thus, through the Holy Bible, God has spoken to mankind.

Enlightenment: The Supreme Authority

This passage is from the second Chapter, the 46th Stanza:

"The sage who knows God has as little need for the Scriptures as one might have for a pond when the whole land is covered in flood."

Commentary

Spiritually unenlightened human beings, whose approach to God is through the doorway of the Scriptures, imagine divine truth always framed in that opening. Nor can they easily relate to any other approach.

Thus, when a great master comes on earth and teaches from his own vast and forever fresh vision of reality, their first question of him is: "To what Scriptural authority are you appealing?"

The Gospel of St. John probably refers to the vastness of the truth revealed by Jesus, and not only to his deeds (which after all could only have been finite in number), when it ends with the words: "And there are also many other things which Jesus did, the which, if they should be written every one, I suppose that even the world itself could not contain the books that should be written."

Most religious believers the world over identify divine Truth with what is written in their scriptures. Orthodox Christians, for example, speak of the Bible as the word of God — the implication being that everything God ever wanted to say to mankind is contained in that book. One recent defender of the faithful even went so far as to count up the number of words in the King James translation of the New Testament, and to announce that, because this was a divine number, the Bible was thereby proved conclusively to be the word of God. Only God Himself, the writer insisted, could have been so exact!

Dogmatic Hindus, similarly, quote their scriptures in supposedly final support of their own limited understanding of the truth, or to disprove the inspired teachings of living masters.

The truth, however, is something to be experienced in itself, and not merely experienced vicariously through reading the Bhagavad Gita or the Holy Bible. That is why Jesus said, "If ye continue in my word, then are ye my disciples indeed; *And ye shall know the truth*, and the truth shall make you free." (John 8:31,32)

One must, of course, start with what one knows,

and with what one is capable of understanding. To one with no spiritual realization, the Scriptures may be the only reliable point of reference. Every religious believer, however, should understand that no *definition* of truth, however divinely inspired, can fully take the place of the truth itself. A definition is not the reality that it defines. Religion must be lived. Its verities must be experienced, and not merely debated.

There is always, and quite understandably, the fear in orthodox religion that false prophets, claiming direct personal experience of God, might promulgate heresies that will undermine people's understanding of the Scriptures. Organized religion therefore erects ramparts against teachings of any kind that are not already endorsed by its official dogmas.

This barrier against false teachings becomes also, unfortunately, a barrier against fresh, true inspiration.

God's way, on the other hand, is ever to create life anew. Every springtime, new flowers grow. Every autumn, new crops are harvested. In winter, no two snowflakes are exactly alike.

God's truth, too, is infinite. It manifests itself ever afresh through the lives of those saints who commune with Him in their souls.

How can the devotee protect himself against false teachings while yet remaining open to the freshness of divine inspiration? For without such openness, spirituality itself becomes blocked.

If we can train our minds to approach truth as a mustard seed (to use the concept offered by Jesus), which grows and spreads to become a mighty tree, then will our understanding of the Scriptures at least be humble. We need to be able to say to ourselves, when we read the Scriptures, "This much at least I have understood. May God enlighten me that my understanding continually grow."

When new teachers appear on earth, as Krishna did, and Jesus, and Buddha, with new explanations of divine truths, how should we respond to them?

We should accept the possibility that they may be speaking from levels of realization to which we ourselves have not yet attained.

We should then, as Jesus suggested, judge them "by their fruits."

We should also apply to them the test of Scripture, for if in fact their teaching contradicts scriptural teachings, it cannot be true.

Even false teachers, however, may side correctly with the teachings of the Scriptures, and yet delude their followers, particularly if their aim is to draw people to themselves instead of to God.

The important thing is to give both truth and fallacy sufficient time to reveal themselves for what they are; and not, in the name of religious purity (but actually in a spirit of fanatical hysteria), to persecute them.

As the wise doctor of Jewish law, Gamaliel, said to those orthodox Jews who wanted to persecute the early Christians, "Let them alone: for if this teaching and this work be of men, it will come to nothing. But if it be of God, you cannot suppress it: lest perchance you find yourselves standing in opposition to God." (Acts 5:38,39)

God's truth is like a vast ocean in which all the Scriptures of the world are like drops. Let us, if we would attain true wisdom, use Scripture as a guideline to reality, but never as a substitute for it.

And thus, through the Bhagavad Gita, God has spoken to mankind.

Week 11

Reason vs. Intuition

Bible

Intuition: The Foundation Stone

This passage is from the Gospel of St. Matthew, Chapter 16, Verses 13-18:

"When Jesus arrived at the district of Caesarea Philippi, he asked his disciples, 'Who do people say that I the Son of man am?' And they replied, 'Some say thou art John the Baptist: some, Elijah; and others, Jeremiah, or one of the other prophets.'

"Then he asked them further, 'But who do you say that I am?'

"And Simon Peter replied, 'Thou art the Christ, the son of the living God.'

"And Jesus turned to him, saying, 'Blessed art thou, Simon, son of Jonah: for not by human nature was this truth revealed to thee, but by my heavenly Father. And I tell thee this also: Thou art Peter, which is to say, a rock, and upon this rock will I build my church, and never will the powers of darkness overwhelm it.'"

Commentary

We see here beautifully contrasted two fundamental ways for arriving at a truth: human reason
on the one hand; and the soul-faculty of intuition on
the other. The people around Jesus witnessed the
many miracles he performed; they probably felt also
his extraordinary magnetism and love, and sensed
the divine authority in his presence. They therefore
realized — indeed, with some degree of intuition
too, since their measure of him must have been
based partly on their inner feelings — that here was
no common man. Who, they seem to have been ask-
ing themselves, could this extraordinary individual
be?

And then human reason took over, and they
tried to identify Jesus with someone about whom
something was known already: John the Baptist,
perhaps, or one of the ancient prophets.

Such is reason's way: Instead of breaking new
ideational ground, it tries to relate every new fact to
something that is already familiar. New conclusions
arrived at by reason alone will always be seen, on
close inspection, to have been constructed — often
most painstakingly — out of an assortment of mate-
rials already to hand.

That which introduces fresh, new insights into
human understanding is the faculty of intuition.
Great minds are always distinguished by this intuitive ability. Often, their extraordinary insights defy
the most insistent conclusions of logic. No one else
seems quite to understand how those insights were
arrived at. Yet it is commonly accepted that the as-

tonishing success of such people, whatever their chosen fields, is due especially to this intuitive faculty.

Intuition is a soul-faculty. Paramhansa Yogananda defined it as "the soul's power of knowing God." Its insights flow downward into the conscious mind — filtered, often, by the mist of human preconceptions — from the superconsciousness.

It is intuition, for example, which accounts for Einstein's far-from-expected discovery of the law of relativity — a realization that took him many years, subsequently, to justify to other scientists by the laborious process of reason.

St. Teresa of Avila said that, in a state of ecstasy, the soul recognizes in a flash truths which reason may require many years to learn.

The conscious mind, indeed, can do no other than *learn* new truths: It cannot recognize them. Recognition of truths that are not revealed to the mind by the senses is specifically the function of intuition.

All those who recognized something of the divinity in Jesus, and whose recognition made them ask themselves who this man might really be, probably felt, as we said, some stirrings of soul-intuition within themselves. Peter's intuitive faculties, however, were more perfectly developed than theirs. His deep inner communion with the Lord enabled him clearly to recognize in Jesus no mere prophet, but the very Messiah, the living Christ.

Jesus announced that Peter had arrived at this conclusion not by the deductions of reason (as those had done who speculated that Jesus might be one of the ancient prophets), but by inner revelation from God — that is to say, by deep soul-intuition.

Reason, often, is unreliable in the search for truth. If its premise is wrong, any deductions drawn from that premise will be wrong also. Deductions even from right premises may be influenced by un-examined and erroneous assumptions. Many times has the most carefully constructed framework of logic collapsed like a house of cards before the mer-est puff of breeze from some newly discovered fact.

Intuition, however, when firmly rooted in soul-consciousness, is as reliable as the clear certainty within the hearts of every one of us that we exist. It was to the lack of this faculty that Jesus referred when he said (John 8:43), "Why do ye not under-stand my speech? even because ye cannot hear my word."

And it was in recognition of this bedrock of intui-tive perception in Peter that Jesus said to him, "Thou art Peter, which is to say, a rock."

On that bedrock of spiritual awareness, he con-tinued, he would build his church. Paramhansa Yogananda explained that, by church, Jesus meant the mystical "edifice" of cosmic consciousness. Pe-ter, in other words, had demonstrated his spiritual preparedness to receive the supreme gift Jesus had to bestow: that of God-realization.

We do not find Jesus discussing elsewhere the foundation of a church in his name. On the other hand, we find him saying, "Destroy this temple, and in three days I will raise it up." (John 2:19) On that occasion, we learn, his reference was not to the temple at Jerusalem, but to his own body. Many of his other allusions to material things were likewise symbolic. He said, for example, in John 4:32, "I have meat to eat that ye know not of," when by meat he meant something very different from what his disciples assumed.

Even granting tradition's claim, namely, that Jesus was prophesying that Peter would found a new religion in his name, the important point would be that such a new religion would base its strength on the bedrock of realized wisdom, and not on the fragile sands of intellectually conceived dogmas.

It is high time, in the historical unfoldment of religious teaching, for sincere seekers to develop their own ability to recognize truth — not by common sense only, nor by abstract logic, but by the intuitive powers of the soul. For science has conditioned us not to remain satisfied with belief alone. It is time, therefore, that we did more than believe in God. We must commune with Him!

The "church" of God is, as St. Paul put it in II Corinthians, 5:1, "A house not made with hands, eternal in the heavens."

Thus, through the Holy Bible, God has spoken to mankind.

Bhagavad Gita

Communion With the Inner Silence

This passage is from the second Chapter, the 53rd Stanza:

> *"When your intellect, at present confused by the diversity of teaching in the Scriptures, becomes steadfast in the ecstasy of deep meditation, then you will achieve final union with God."*

Commentary

The Bhagavad Gita implies here that any search for spiritual truth, without the corresponding practice of deep, inner communion, will probably result sooner or later in mental confusion. For even the simplest teachings are open to misinterpretation.

The basic concern of the Scriptures, therefore, is only secondarily with defining truths, or with formulating dogmas. Spiritual niceties of this sort are more appropriately left to the pedants. The Scriptures, on the other hand, are more concerned with sounding a call to spiritual action. They offer practical suggestions for how one may grow in the actual realization of truth. And they seek to inspire in all men the desire to tread this highest path.

Endless theorizing is for labyrinthine minds. More pleasing to God than all the scholarship that human brain can hold is a heart, even though the mind be unlettered, that is open to His love.

The way to know God is by stilling the mind, and not by agitating it: by deep meditation, and not by reasoning intricately from countless Scriptural premises.

The way to know God is by living consciously in His blissful presence, and not by the perfunctory performance of outward rituals.

The way to know God, finally, is to commune with Him in inner silence, with true love, and not to shout to the heavens the carefully reasoned dogmas of one's beliefs.

He who loves deeply will speak little to others of his love. But he who boasts proudly of his devotion, and with outward noise displays his piety to others, is too besotted with the "music" of his own voice ever to hear the silent whispers of the infinite Beloved in his soul.

Dear ones, let us speak little, but love greatly. And let us ever commune with God in the ecstatic silence of our own souls.

Thus, through the Bhagavad Gita, God has spoken to mankind.

Is Heaven Man's Birthright?

Bible

We Are Children of the Light

This passage is from the Gospel of St. John, Chapter 3, the 13th Verse:

> *"No man hath ascended up to heaven but him that came down from heaven; [even so] the Son of man who is in heaven."*

Commentary

Is Jesus saying here that no one but him ever ascended to heaven? Or was his use, rather, of the past tense intended to mean that, while those who lived before him hadn't ascended to heaven, from now on heaven would be open to all those who acknowledged him?

It is, certainly, far from the spirit of all of his other teachings for him to claim that no one but him would ever ascend to heaven. Often he spoke of people going there. Even to one of the criminals who were crucified with him, he said, "Verily I say unto thee, *this day* shalt thou be with me in paradise." (Luke 23:43)

As for his use of the past tense, he said (Matthew 8:11): "Many... shall sit down with Abraham, and Isaac, and Jacob in the kingdom of heaven." Clearly his meaning here is that three, at least, of the ancient prophets had been welcomed into heaven.

What this passage offers, then, is a simple but important truth. As the ancient philosopher Plotinus put it: "Like only can comprehend like."

Jesus here is explaining how it is possible for human beings to ascend to heaven — and, by extension, to know Truth. How? Because it is from heaven that we have all descended! We are children of God, of His light; and not — except in the blindness of our material delusion — the offspring of darkness and sin.

Jesus differed from unenlightened mortals in that he had descended from that realm consciously. He spoke from his own experience. As he put it to Nicodemus, prior to the passage quoted above: "Verily, verily, I say unto thee, We speak that which we do know, and testify that which we have seen."

Jesus was underscoring the authority with which he spoke when he referred to "the Son of Man who *is* in heaven." A great master lives consciously in the astral realm, even as he does on this material plane of existence. Communication is as easy and natural for him with the inhabitants of that world as it is for the people of this one.

Heaven, in this passage, refers to the higher regions of the astral universe — that world which exists behind the gross atoms of the material universe. The astral universe is a vast region of light and energy — similar in appearance, though not in substance, to the world around us. In fact, the entire physical universe is only a projection of that subtler level of universal creation.

Man's physical body, too, is a projection of his astral body, which in fact it resembles. When in death he abandons his earthly form, he goes on living in his astral body, and in the astral world. There, he continues to experience whatever predominant state of consciousness he created for himself while on earth. The major difference between the astral world and this world is that, there, his awareness is no longer enclosed in the dense cocoon of matter. Whatever he experiences after death of happiness or misery is, consequently, intensified.

If, while on earth, he expressed kindness to others, and loved God, his joy in the heavenly world is extreme. But if on earth he lived selfishly, and acknowledged no other reality than his own, after death he will find himself abandoned in his ego, and utterly alone. Discovering nothing external on which to feed his egoic desires, because hemmed in by the fog of self-involvement, he may see nothing anywhere but darkness, and may therefore experience only fear and suffering.

Jesus' statement in this verse makes it clear also that man's physical body could not survive in the subtle astral realms. It is in his astral body that he ascends to heaven: that which "came down from heaven." Jesus, however, awake as he was in God, could maintain uninterrupted his conscious identity as the Son of man — that is to say, as a human being — while living simultaneously as an angelic being in the astral world. Thus, he was able to speak of his body as being even then in heaven.

It is important to realize that heaven is man's divine birthright. As children of Light, darkened though our vision be by our attachment to matter, there is a center deep within each of us where divine Truth can be recognized.

Meditate, then, whenever you read the Bible. Hold the words up to God's holy presence within you, and to your own superconsciousness. For you have potentially the power, if you choose to develop it, to attain the heavenly heights. Remember always: It is from those heights that your soul descended to earth.

At the same time, be humble. Know that, as you have the potential to develop your own latent spirituality, so there must be others who even now are more spiritually developed than you — masters, too, who can say with Jesus, "We speak that which we do know, and testify that which we have seen."

With humility, such as true saints have shown, you will behold the sun of divine awakening rising gradually in the firmament of your consciousness. Then will every shadow of doubt be dispelled from your heart.

Thus, through the Holy Bible, God has spoken to mankind.

Bhagavad Gita

"Like Only Can Comprehend Like"

This passage is from the fifteenth Chapter, the 11th Stanza:

"Seekers of union with the Lord find Him dwelling in their own hearts. But those who, lacking in wisdom, seek Him with impure motives, cannot perceive Him however much they struggle to do so."

Commentary

Here the Bhagavad Gita is saying that we must seek God with no other desire than union with Him. The ancient philosopher Plotinus said, "Like only can comprehend like." God is the Lord of Love. Only through pure, self-giving love for Him can we know Him. This, again, is the deeper meaning of the

Biblical commandment, "Thou shalt have no other gods before Me."

Many superficial devotees imagine that because the Scriptures say we are the children of God, they need only affirm this truth mentally to experience it fully in themselves. The kingdom of God is not for such spiritual dilettantes.

Those who do not try to follow the rules of moral conduct, and who practice yoga methods without deep interest and devotion, will not receive the spiritual benefits they look for.

Many students of yoga perform the techniques in a haphazard way; then wonder why they do not "get anywhere," and why they fail to feel communion with the Infinite even after apparently serious meditation. Scriptural statements to the effect that we have come from God are meant to encourage and inspire us to exert ourselves with zeal. They are certainly not meant to lull us with false reassurances regarding our present realities! As long as we give prime importance to the ego, and follow even the spiritual path for motives other than perfect union with God, we must remain in delusion.

Heavenly happiness in God, so the Scriptures solemnly declare, is our divine birthright. But we must diligently, unsparingly, and with deep attention remove the rust of egoism and self-seeking from the mirror of our consciousness, if we would find the Lord's ever-shining presence reflected there.

Thus, through the Bhagavad Gita, God has spoken to mankind.

Imperfection Is of the Ego; Perfection, of the Soul

Bible

Living in God's Love

This passage is from the Gospel of St. Matthew, Chapter 5, the 21st and 22nd Verses:

"You have heard that our forefathers were told, 'Thou shalt not kill'; and again, 'Whoever kills shall be subject to condemnation.' But my message to you is this: Whoever is angry with his brother without cause already stands condemned; whoever contemptuously calls his brother a fool shall answer for it to the Supreme Council; and whoever calls his brother an outcast of God shall be in danger of hellfire."

Commentary

There are many forms of murder. Killing the body is only the most visible form. But to kill a person's belief in himself, or — even worse — to destroy his faith in God: This is a much more insidious form of murder, and one far more hateful in the eyes of God.

Many self-proclaimed believers imagine that the Lord is pleased with them when they self-righteously condemn others as sinners and spiritual outcasts. Jesus, however, forever offered hope even to the worst of sinners. He emphasized not the darkness of their sin, but their eternal potential, as children of God, to return to the light.

In the famous story of the woman taken in adultery, he told her simply, "Go, and sin no more."

Worse than physical murder, which denies another person's right to live, is the sin of suicide, which denies life itself. Worse, again, than the condemnation of others as sinful is to condemn *oneself* as a sinner. For by condemning oneself, one denies the very saving power of grace. As Paramhansa Yogananda used to say, "The worst sin is to call yourself a sinner!"

There is the story of an occasion when Yogananda attended a Gospel "revival" meeting. At a certain point in the proceedings, the preacher shouted at his congregation, "You are all sinners: Get down on your knees!" Yogananda remarked later, "I looked around me, and found I was the only one who wasn't kneeling! I wouldn't join them, because I wouldn't accept that I was a sinner."

It is an irony of human nature that, in our judgment of others, we judge ourselves. If we hate weakness in others, it is because there exists in ourselves, too, some weakness of which we are ashamed. If we hate others for their pride, it is because on some level our own pride gives us discomfort. And if we condemn others as sinners, it is because, somewhere deep within us, we fear that we, too, may not be living in God's grace.

From love for God, faith is born. Charity towards others nurtures love for God. If we judge others kindly, we will feel God's kindliness and grace in our own hearts. Jesus put it beautifully in the beatitude: "Blessed are the merciful, for they shall obtain mercy."

To live close to God, we must see Him as our loving Father, never as a wrathful Judge. He is our very own. The approach to Him is, for everyone who awakens in Him, an act of recognition. The prodigal son returns at last to his divine home, where alone he has ever belonged.

Live, therefore, in God's love. He will guide you on the path of righteousness, until you achieve final union with Him.

For thus, through the Holy Bible, God has spoken to mankind.

Author's note: The above translation includes a phrase that is found in some texts, but not in all. These other translations omit the important phrase, "outcast of God." Jesus, however, had a good reason for including it. It strengthens, and does not essentially change, the meaning of the entire passage as it has been captured by all the translators.

Bhagavad Gita

Live at Your Divine Center

This passage is from the second Chapter, the 20th Stanza:

"This Self is never born, nor does it perish. Once existing, it cannot ever cease to be. It is birthless, eternal, changeless, ever itself. It is not slain when the body is killed."

Commentary

The Self here referred to, obviously, is not that self which one sees every morning in the mirror while combing his hair! Man tends to confuse his human body and personality with deeper realities of his being. Immortality, for many believers, means living through all eternity as essentially the same person: holier than now, perhaps, but with the ego and personality, and even the body, more or less intact. Joe Green exalted in heavenly glory is imagined as Joe Green wearing a big smile, as he wanders endlessly through green pastures playing a harp of gold.

In the Bible we find an instructive episode: "Then there arose a dispute among [the disciples] as to which of them was the greatest. Jesus, knowing what was passing in their minds, took a child and stood him at his side. 'Whoever receives this child in my name,' he said, 'receives me. And whoever receives me receives the One who sent me. For whoever is least among all of you is the greatest.'" (Luke 9:46-48)

In another Bible passage, St. John the Baptist says of Christ: "He must increase, but I must decrease." (John 3:30) Understood in its deepest sense, as St. John's Gospel always needs to be understood, the meaning here, clearly, is this: "To live in spiritual perfection, the Christ consciousness in us must increase; but it can do so only to the extent that the ego decreases in importance for us."

When we read in the Scriptures of the soul's divine potential as a child of God, we must understand that this high promise altogether excludes the ego. The ego is a role assumed only temporarily by the soul. It is *the soul*, as Paramhansa Yogananda defined it, *attached to the body*.

To know God, we must abandon the last vestiges of ego-consciousness. As Jesus put it in Luke 17:33, "Whosoever shall seek to save his life shall lose it; and whosoever shall lose his life shall save it, and live." The eternal life promised to mankind in the

Scriptures is that of eternal joy in God. This divine life he cannot have so long as he clings to his little ego, like a drowning man to a straw.

To achieve the greater, he must be willing to relinquish the lesser. Such, indeed, is the prerequisite for even normal, worldly success.

The body undergoes life's normal changes; and yet, inwardly, one remains the same person. One acquires new attributes of personality, yet there remains within him a center of self-awareness that doesn't change with the personality. We define ourselves in terms of appearances, yet on analysis, we see that these definitions are false, because fleeting. Like peeling an onion, if one by one we strip away such definitions, what do we have left in the end? Nothing! That is to say, *no thing*: nothing solid; nothing definable in any limiting terms.

What is left is that Self which is never born, which never perishes, which remains forever changeless, forever itself. Weapons cannot destroy it, though they destroy the body. Death cannot destroy it, though it destroy the brain. The Self is behind the brain, using it as one uses a computer. The Self cannot ever be affected.

Know that *that*, eternally, is what you are. Sri Krishna, in this passage of the Bhagavad Gita, is telling us to live ever more deeply at our divine center within, and not to define ourselves superficially, which is to say, in any outward context. We are not sinners. We are not the greater for any human virtue. Again and again in the Scriptures we find the admonition to attribute all glory to God, and to realize that in Him alone can we have our own glory.

Thus, through the Bhagavad Gita, God has spoken to mankind.

Easter Sunday

*Supplement — To be inserted into sequence
wherever Easter Sunday occurs.*

Week 14

Easter

The Resurrection — and the Meaning of Divine Tests

Bible

The Divine Treasure Must Be Earned

This passage is from the Gospel of St. John, Chapter 20, the 1st, 2nd, and 19th Verses:

> "The first day of the week cometh Mary Magdalene early, when it was yet dark, unto the sepulchre, and seeth the stone taken away from the sepulchre.
>
> "Then she runneth, and cometh to Simon Peter, and to the other disciple, whom Jesus loved, and saith unto them, They have taken away the Lord!...
>
> "Then the same day at evening, being the first day of the week, when the doors were shut where

the disciples were assembled for fear of the Jews, came Jesus and stood in their midst, and saith unto them, Peace be unto you."

Commentary

Countless are the lessons to be found in Jesus' crucifixion and resurrection. All of them relate in one way or another to our own resurrection in God, and to God's grace as the means of effecting such transformation in us.

Ideally — at least from the human point of view! — resurrection should not have to be preceded by tests of any kind, let alone by such a tragedy as the crucifixion! Why, the ego asks, can we not ascend to God in easy stages, wafted upward pleasantly on gentle breezes of ecstatic inspiration?

St. Teresa of Avila, after a spiritual test — the latest in a lifetime of them — had a vision of Jesus, who told her, "Don't feel badly, Teresa. This is how I treat all my friends."

"Ah, my Lord," replied St. Teresa, "That is why you have so few!"

The wrongs we have done in life must sooner or later be paid for. Our mistakes must be righted. Isn't it better that they be righted while we are still here on earth? For then, when the time comes for us to leave this world, we shall enter the other one in a state of freedom.

Jesus said, "He that taketh not his cross, and followeth after me, is not worthy of me." (Matthew 10:38)

Indeed, simply to live on earth is to take up the

cross of material existence, with its myriad burdens of fatigue, hunger, limitation, and pain. Mankind is forever subject to suffering. Injustice and cruelty, in one form or another, are the common lot of all humanity. Sorrow and happiness, in repeated succession, make up the endless procession of life.

Mankind generally, however, has no understanding of why it is that he suffers. He sees himself as the innocent victim of a blind and indifferent destiny, or of hostile forces against which he must ever try to defend or revenge himself. Never holding his suffering up to the light of a higher wisdom, but always blaming it on "bad luck," or on others' unfairness to him, he learns at best only indirectly from whatever tests life sends him.

The devotee, on the other hand, who sincerely offers his life, with all its tests and fulfillments, up to God, finds that every test accepted with faith is followed by a marked increase of inner freedom, and by deepened understanding. He learns at last to see in every trial only God's grace, never His punishment.

The cross of tribulation is necessary for mankind, if man would attain the resurrection. Not only do the trials life sends us help us to pay off old debts: Accepted with understanding, they teach us to focus our love single-pointedly on the only reality where joy is never dimmed: union with God.

The Lord doesn't allow us to learn this lesson cheaply. "The pearl of great price" cannot be paid for with the debased currencies of earth: power, popularity, material success. Often, indeed, God makes us feel that His attention is anywhere but on us and on our tearful prayers to Him.

Thus, too, were the disciples of Jesus tested, when the Master they thought would soon declare himself before all the world in power and great glory was suddenly seized by fools, beaten, infamously judged, and crucified. The disciples' darkest hour followed, when, in fear for their own lives, they assembled. Yet this meeting was held in faith; otherwise, each one would have sought safety separately on his own. They were assembled as disciples.

And suddenly Jesus stood in their midst, and said to them, "Peace be unto you."

In these few, simple words we see the end of every divine test, when accepted with loving faith. No matter how dark the hour, when it ends, if it has been lived for God, comes divine peace, and greater joy than we have ever known before.

> *"Every grief, every wrong*
> *Has its ending in song."*

Those who in grief forget God never learn this lesson. Every devotee, however, who clings to the Lord through every trial and difficulty, finds His Beloved smiling at him at each turn of the road. In every new blessing he finds Easter; in every new grace: the Resurrection.

Thus it is, through the Holy Bible, that God has spoken to mankind.

Bhagavad Gita

God: Man's Eternal Friend

This passage is from the ninth Chapter, Stanzas 33 and 34:

> *"Ah! ye who into this ill world are come —*
> *Fleeting and false — set your faith fast on Me!*
> *Fix heart and thought on Me! Adore Me!*
> *Bring Offerings to Me! Make Me prostrations!*
> *Make Me your supremest joy! and, undivided,*
> *Unto My rest your spirits shall be guided."*

Commentary

Wise alone among mortal men is he whose discernments lead him ever Godward: who, deep within himself, realizes that worldly goals must always disappoint him. For, however bright with promises the world be — like the dewdrops at dawn glistening on a rose — its promises are forever false — even as the illusory dewdrops, which evaporate under the heat of the sun's rays.

God often tests His devotees, by seeming to give them exactly that which they fear the most. It may appear as if He were testing only their endurance. But in fact, what He is testing is their love.

The human tendency, under every blow of adversity, is to close inwardly upon oneself — like the traveler before the fierce onslaughts of a desert sandstorm; or like the tortoise, which at every threat to its safety withdraws protectively into its shell. Time is required for such a person to come out of himself again, to open himself trustingly to life. Many people, after what might even seem like minor tests, remain bitter for the rest of their mortal lives.

God Himself cannot help us, if we enclose ourselves protectively within self-erected walls of our egos, and if we turn away suspiciously whenever He stretches out his hand to us with love. Many devotees, tested by God, misunderstand the subtle workings of His grace, and lose faith in Him. To such foolish ones, God ever whispers silently in their souls, "I will wait. Eventually, you will understand how eternally deep My love is for you."

But the person of true devotion, whose faith remains joyful and unwavering, embraces every test God sends him with arms outstretched to receive it. He lovingly believes that any trial is as much his heavenly Father's gift to him as other experiences which might come to him more attractively wrapped! For such a devotee, always, those very storms of life which seem to bode the worst calamities prove to be but the nourishing rain clouds of God's blessings in the end.

Such is the experience of every true seeker. God is our infinite Beloved. He is our Friend. He wishes us perfect happiness, and peace. His tests are meant only to help us, and instruct us. The sooner we learn to accept them with faith in His good will for us — accept them out of our own love for Him — the sooner we discover that, should He even summon us to walk through fire, the fire will not burn us. Its flames, rather, will soothe our every pain; they will burn away all our impurities, which for so long have been the cause of so much suffering.

Have faith in the Lord. Love Him above everything else! Surrender to Him. Give Him your heart. Open yourself to Him — especially in your darkest hours. For the Lord alone — never the glistening dewdrops of earthly lures! — can give you the peace for which your soul so long has craved.

And thus, through the Bhagavad Gita, God has spoken to mankind.

Part III

The Soul's Ascent

"He must increase, but I must decrease."
— St. John the Baptist, John 3:30

What Does it Mean, To Believe?

Bible

Man Must Live His Beliefs

This passage is from the Gospel of St. John, Chapter 3, Verses 16-21:

"For God so loved the world, that he gave his only begotten Son, that whosoever believeth in him should not perish, but have everlasting life. For God sent not his Son into the world to condemn the world; but that the world through him might be saved.

"He that believeth on him is not condemned: but he that believeth not is condemned already, because he hath not believed in the name of the only begotten Son of God.

"And this is the condemnation: That light is come into the world, and men loved darkness rather than light, because their deeds were evil. For every one that doeth evil hateth the light, nei-

ther cometh to the light, lest his deeds should be reproved.   But he that doeth truth cometh to the light, that his deeds may be made manifest, that they are wrought in God."

Commentary

In earlier readings we explored the meaning of this expression: "the only begotten Son." To repeat briefly what we said: God, who created the universe, known now to consist of hundreds of billions of galaxies, cannot easily be imagined as having begotten, uniquely in all the universe, one single offspring on this tiny planet, our earth.

Spiritual truths are often veiled in symbolism, with the purpose of forcing us to dig beneath their surface in our efforts to understand them. For the sake of our own spiritual growth, we need to reach out and touch them on their own level of reality.

Jesus' divine status as the Son of God is commonly attributed to his miraculous birth. But Jesus himself said, "Before Abraham was, *I am.*" (John 8:58) Jesus the man was born of Mary. Christ, the infinite consciousness, however, with which Jesus' consciousness was identified, existed already in eternity, eons of time before his human birth; before the birth of Abraham — before the very creation of the galaxies.

The expression, "the only begotten," so Paramhansa Yogananda explained, refers to the universal reflection in creation of God the Father, beyond creation.

This is a profound truth. But should it prove too

deep for many seekers, whose present need is to know what step to take next on the spiritual path, the point is not immediately crucial. It is enough for most Christians simply to believe deeply in Jesus. Deep faith in him, as a true incarnation of God, will certainly lead them to progressively deeper insights into the eternal verities.

The essential teaching in these words of Jesus, therefore, concerns belief: "Whosoever *believeth* in him shall have everlasting life." What, in the sense here intended, does it mean to believe?

Jesus himself said in Matthew 7:21, "Not every one that saith unto me, Lord, Lord, shall enter into the kingdom of heaven; but he that *doeth* the will of my Father, which is in heaven."

The students of many a great artist have believed in him implicitly, in his theories, in his methods. This fact alone hasn't necessarily made them good artists. Many art lovers, again, have argued heatedly the merits of one school of art over those of another, without themselves being capable of producing a single worthwhile painting.

The worthy student, whatever his chosen field, labors incessantly, out of the depth of his faith, to attune himself to the realities he is trying to express. The sincere violin student practices again and again until he can place his fingers on the strings in exactly those positions which will produce the right notes. To produce a true tone, as any violinist will confirm, is not easy.

The opera student repeats vocal exercises for years, that he may learn well how to produce his notes with maximum carrying power.

Whatever one's subject, one who really believes in it will never stop short of achieving mastery. Were he to be satisfied with mediocrity, it would indicate some defect in his own belief.

Jesus made it very clear in this passage that what he meant by belief was, as he put it, *"doing truth"* — that is, *living* the truth. Next, he said, believing means *"coming to the light."*

Every action, every thought, every feeling that is not in tune with the light of truth, which *is* Christ, constitutes an insufficiency of acceptance, of sincere belief. One who accepts sincerely does so in order to become changed, to grow spiritually, and not to parade before the world his outward affiliation with this religion or with that.

God, Jesus said, does not condemn us if we refuse His light. We condemn ourselves, by turning our backs on the light, and by electing instead to live in self-perpetuating darkness.

It is true also that if we reject *any* divine channel — as the followers of one religion often do the truths expressed in other religions — to that extent we reject also God. In this sense, we condemn ourselves to tunnel vision, which is a relative kind of darkness. God is not pleased by sectarianism. His love is infinite. In sending down to earth a ray of His light, He would have us expand our experience of that light to infinity.

Let us, then, lift up our hearts in gratitude to Him who has sent His one light repeatedly into the world for the salvation of humanity. And let our acceptance of that light be not with our minds only, but with our entire being. Let us love God, as Jesus would have us do, with all our heart, mind, soul, and strength.

Then indeed shall we not perish in ignorance, but have eternal life in God.

Thus, through the Holy Bible, God has spoken to mankind.

Bhagavad Gita

How To Grow in Wisdom

This passage is from the twelfth Chapter, Stanzas 8-11:

"Cling thou to Me!
Clasp Me with heart and mind! so shalt thou dwell
Surely with Me on high. But if thy thought
Droops from such height; if thou be'st weak to set
Body and soul upon Me constantly,
Despair not! give Me lower service! seek
To reach Me, worshipping with steadfast will;
And, if thou canst not worship steadfastly,
Work for Me, toil in works pleasing to Me!
For he that laboureth right for love of Me
Shall finally attain! But, if in this
Thy faint heart fails, bring Me thy failure!"

Commentary

Paramhansa Yogananda wrote, concerning the modes of liberation here suggested, that they are what make the precepts of the Bhagavad Gita "so sweet, sympathetic, and useful in healing the manifold sicknesses of suffering humanity."

There is no room, indeed, in all God's Truth for judgment. We are His children, students in a School of Life where He has placed us that we might learn.

It takes time to grow in understanding. Not everyone by any means has reached a point in his spiritual evolution where it is possible for him to offer one-pointed devotion and love to God. A St. Francis of Assisi, or a St. Teresa of Avila, is that rarest of flowers among mankind: an almost-perfected being. Most people must struggle with varying degrees of spiritual confusion in themselves: habitual indifference, dullness, negativity, doubt.

How is the average person, enmeshed in a web of restless thoughts and desires, to obey sincerely the commandment of God in the Bhagavad Gita, "Cling thou to Me!"? or that of Jesus in the Bible, to love God with all one's heart, mind, soul, and strength?

Both the Bhagavad Gita and the Holy Bible take into account that there are many grades in this great School of Life. Truth is indeed absolute, but the pathway to it is winding and long. Those who, while climbing the trail to the summit, find themselves as yet far down the mountainside, need something besides absolutes to inspire them. They need teachings that will be relevant to where they presently find themselves on the path.

The soul, in its long labors to achieve divine perfection, needs not only the freedom to advance according to its own natural ability, but also the freedom to make its own mistakes. Without mistakes, indeed, we might never really learn any lesson thoroughly.

No one can understand the evils of drinking so well as one who has himself experienced the suffering that accompanies alcoholism. No one is so dedicated to healing the physical ailments of others as one who, in the past, through abuse of his own body, suffered physical illness himself. And no one feels as much compassion for the insane as one who once knew insanity himself.

Man doesn't need judgment in his efforts to develop spiritually. He needs encouragement. He needs practical guidance. He needs help!

That is why Jesus says in the Gospel of John, Chapter 3: "For God sent not his Son into the world to condemn the world; but that the world through him might be saved." It is why he said also, to the woman taken in adultery, "Neither do I condemn thee."

We condemn ourselves, if in our ignorance we turn our backs on the light, and close our eyes. But even this is not so much a condemnation as it is a temporary mistake. No one wants to suffer. Nor, certainly, does God want us to suffer. He has, however, made us in His own image of perfect Joy, and whenever we fail to act in harmony with that image, we inevitably experience pain. Once we realize that the cause of our suffering lies in ourselves, we find ourselves challenged by our own discrimination to begin the slow, often painful labor of correcting that cause, and of returning to the light — to the high place where we belong.

The Bhagavad Gita tells us not to worry unduly over our imperfections, but to do what we can with the positive qualities we have already to hand. God is eternally patient. "Rome," as the saying goes, "wasn't built in a day." And: "A saint," as Yogananda often said, "is a sinner who never gave up!"

Thus, through the Bhagavad Gita, God has spoken to mankind.

All Human Qualities, Even Virtues, Must Be Transcended

Bible

God Alone Is the Doer

The passage this week is from the Gospel of St. Matthew, Chapter 5, Verse 20:

> *"I say unto you, That except your righteousness shall exceed the righteousness of the scribes and Pharisees, ye shall in no case enter into the kingdom of heaven."*

Commentary

Contrast Jesus' statement here with another one by St Paul: "For by grace are ye saved through faith; and that not of yourselves: it is the gift of God: Not of works, lest any man should boast." (Ephesians 2:8,9)

Are these two quotations as mutually contradictory as they seem? Jesus, certainly, is exhorting his disciples to heroic efforts. What he is saying, in effect, is: "Don't be satisfied with standard definitions of spirituality, but seek perfection in God. Look for His approval, not for the approval of man."

Only a few verses later, indeed, Jesus says: "Be ye therefore perfect, even as your Father which is in heaven is perfect."

St. Paul, on the other hand, seems at first glance to be recommending total dependence on grace, and avoidance of spiritual practices of any kind. People often quote these words of his, in fact, to justify a more or less haphazard approach to spirituality.

What St. Paul is really saying is that we should do everything in the consciousness of God's guiding presence within, and not allow ourselves to be motivated by the compulsive desires of the ego. As the seldom-quoted sequel to St. Paul's statement puts it, "For we are God's handiwork, created in Christ Jesus *to devote ourselves to the good deeds* for which God has designed us."

St. Paul's words are in fact a ringing call to true Christians to embrace the same kind of spiritual heroism as that to which Jesus exhorted his disciples.

For persons of averagely pious inclination do their alms "before men," as Jesus put it, "to be seen of them." (Matthew 6:1) They seek rather the approval of their fellow religionists than that of God.

How can our righteousness exceed that of the scribes and Pharisees? Never by striving to outshine them in the eyes of others! And never by whipping ourselves to ever greater heights of human virtue, through religiously observing every outward rule and ritual. Even virtue, if it is rooted in the thought, "How virtuous am I!" will keep us firmly chained to the prison walls of ignorance. Our righteousness can exceed that of ordinary religionists only if it springs from the soul, not from the ego.

We must see God alone as the Doer. We must invite Him to act through us, to think through us, to love others through us, to inspire us in every way. Our limited human righteousness must be surrendered at the feet of Infinite Truth; it must become *His* righteousness, not our own. God's is the Truth which, as Jesus said, will make us free.

Humility, however, as Paramhansa Yogananda used to say with a smile, is not a "put-up job." Every religious follower who knows anything at all of the Scriptures knows that they list humility among the chief virtues. It is therefore not unusual for even the Pharisee-type of religionist to pay lip service to this virtue; to claim to act not of himself, but as the humblest servant of God. It can even be good to make such statements, provided one's purpose in making them is only to affirm, and not to impress others.

Affirmation, however, is not the same thing as actual wisdom. To see God really as the Doer, one must clearly perceive His presence in oneself — as a loving Presence, or as a great Light, or a bursting Joy.

To achieve this transcendental awareness, and to cease living on a level of egoic limitations, it is necessary also to do something else that the Pharisees in every religion fail to do: not only pray to God, but *listen* for His answer. For how can we approach God's holy presence, if we do all the talking?

There is a fine line of discrimination here, one which many devotees fail to perceive. On the one hand, we cannot open ourselves to God's grace if we grasp at it forcefully with our human will. On the other hand, however, we cannot receive it in ourselves if we simply wait for it to come to us. Nothing in the Scriptures counsels such passivity! The entire Bible is a call to spiritual action — that is to say, to the right kind of action; to egoless, God-attuned action. We must be heroes of God, but not heroes in the applauding arena of men.

If we truly love God, we can know Him. It is natural for one who loves to seek communion with his beloved. It would be a very indifferent lover indeed who insisted on making nothing but long-winded soliloquies to the object of his affections! One who seeks communion with the beloved will not fail also to listen — to receive — to absorb.

Inner communion with God is essential, if one is really to act in the awareness of His guiding presence and inspiration. Both St. Paul and Jesus told us to live in the actual awareness of that inner Presence — or, as St. Paul put it elsewhere, "by the washing of regeneration, and renewing of the Holy Ghost." (Titus 3:5)

Meditation is the way to inner communion with the Lord. We must use our human will, certainly, but we must use it to set aside our own restless thoughts, our likes and dislikes, and not to affirm them; to open ourselves to God's grace, and to offer ourselves in deep, loving stillness to the Infinite Silence.

In teaching us these truths, God, through the Holy Bible, has spoken to mankind.

Bhagavad Gita

God Alone *Is*

This passage is from the seventh Chapter, the 19th Stanza:

"Yet hard the wise Mahatma is to find,
That man who sayeth, 'All is Vasudev!'"

Commentary

These lines were often quoted by Paramhansa Yogananda, in this poetic translation by Sir Edwin Arnold. *Mahatma* means "great soul," or "sage." *Vasudev* is a name for the Lord. Rare indeed on earth is it to find one who is so merged in the Infinite that, wherever he looks, he sees only God.

The goal of religion is perfect union with the Lord. We were created to drink unceasingly from the "living water" of God's joy. Nor can we ever be fully satisfied until we have fulfilled that destiny. As St. Augustine wrote, "Father, Thou hast made us for Thyself, and our hearts are restless until they find their rest in Thee."

Why are so few people interested in seeking God? Swami Shankara, a great saint two thousand years ago in India, said, "The child is busy with playthings. Youth is busy with sex and romance. The old are busy with sickness and worries. No one is busy with God!"

We are predisposed toward superficiality, toward living at the surface, because from the start of life our energy is drawn outward toward the senses. We must eat; we must relate to others; we must learn to coordinate our body movements; we must learn to communicate. Let's face it, the path to God is an obstacle course! Nature disposes us even before we have any say in the matter to think, "First let me seek my daily bread; only then, maybe, will I have time for my spiritual needs. And anyway, who is this God whom the Scriptures tell me I should worship?"

On the other hand, would it be right for "the pearl of great price" to be for sale at a discount at the local Safeway market? We prize more those things for which we have to work hard, even to suffer.

God knows he has made the course difficult for us. It is wrong to think that He blames us, or, worse still, judges us if every now and then, while running, we fall. Jesus said, "For the Father judgeth no man, but hath committed all judgment unto the Son." (John 5:22) And of the Son's judgment, he said in John 3:17: "For God sent not his Son into the world to condemn the world; but that the world through him might be saved." And finally, two sentences later, he made it clear that condemnation comes from people themselves. We condemn ourselves to darkness by neglecting to open our eyes.

God has all eternity to wait for us. Eventually, we must all come to Him — every one of us. We were created for this glorious destiny alone. Sooner or later, even the slowest learners among us must realize that matter simply cannot give us the lasting happiness we are all seeking.

Our consciousness is refined only gradually, as we discover the superior satisfaction that comes from living by soul values: from giving to others, for example, instead of taking from them. There would not even be any real merit in giving to others, if our true desire were to hoard. God doesn't expect us to do violence to our own actual understanding, any more than a teacher in school, if he is a good one, expects a child to grasp more than he is capable of absorbing. Jesus himself said on the cross, "Forgive them, for they know not what they do."

We have eternity to find God.

We have also, however, eternity to suffer, if we so choose. For the choice to live for ourselves, and not for God, is a choice to live in darkness, and therefore in suffering. In Him alone is true light.

God says elsewhere in the Bhagavad Gita, "Get away from My ocean of suffering and misery!" In *The Hound of Heaven*, a poem by Francis Thompson that Yogananda often quoted, God says to the devotee, "All things forsake thee, who forsakest Me." And such, whether late or soon, is man's discovery. We cannot find the perfect satisfaction we are all seeking, save only in God.

Yogananda often praised an attitude that he found prevalent in America, expressing it thus: "Eventually? Eventually? Why not *now!*"

Let us live *from today* for God. Let us bring Him into everything we do; share with Him our every thought; offer to Him the fruits of all our labors. Thus may we, too, come eventually to look about us and say, "All is Vasudev!"

Thus, through the Bhagavad Gita, God has spoken to mankind.

The Need for
Inner Experience

Bible

"Be Ye Therefore Perfect"

This passage is from the Gospel of St. Matthew, Chapter 5, Verses 43-48:

"Ye have heard that it hath been said, Thou shalt love thy neighbour, and hate thine enemy.

"But I say unto you, Love your enemies; bless them that curse you; do good to them that hate you; and pray for them which despitefully use you, and persecute you;

"That ye may be the children of your Father which is in heaven: for he maketh his sun to rise on the evil and on the good, and sendeth rain on the just and on the unjust.

"For if ye love them which love you, what reward have ye? Do not even the tax collectors the same?

"And if ye salute your brethren only, what do

ye more than others? Do not even the pagans so?
"Be ye therefore perfect, even as your Father
which is in heaven is perfect."

Commentary

Jesus is telling us to live as children of God, and
no longer as children of limitation. He says we
should love everyone with God's perfect, unquali-
fied, unconditional love. These Verses are so inspiring in their message of universal kindness and love
that one might easily overlook their other, deeper
implications.

Let us contemplate the commandment: "Be ye
therefore perfect." For that is quite clearly what Jesus' words are: a commandment. They are more
than advice, and far more than a promise. Jesus was
trying to stir his listeners to fervent action. He was
not merely counseling them to wait in relative passivity for God to fulfill His perfection in them.

Those believers who imagine that God's grace is
given to us human beings without any effort of will
on our own part are answered here forcefully. Jesus
is telling us to strive mightily for perfection, that we
might become worthy of God's grace.

His words are a commandment also not to define
ourselves in terms of our human limitations, of our
human weakness and sinfulness. "Don't accept
human bondage as your reality!" he seems to be urg-
ing us. The common excuse for sinning: "To err is
human," is answered here by Jesus: "Then be *more*
than human! Recognize yourselves as children of
God." We must, he insists, become "perfect, even as

our Father which is in heaven is perfect."

A third, and fundamental, message in these words is this: Jesus was telling us that we can achieve perfection only by God's power, never by our own. For if it were possible for man to become as perfect as God while yet remaining separate from Him, would it not imply the further possibility of an infinite number of supreme godheads? Egoic perfection is a contradiction in terms. The ego is a very definition of imperfection! — and not in its fragility and littleness, merely.

But Jesus made his meaning clear in his earlier commandment: "Live like the children of your Father in heaven." It is from God that we have received the gift of life. Only the power of His divine love can bestow on us the Perfection of Love. For He alone *is* Love.

Jesus is telling us in this vitally important passage that we should transcend the selfish dictates of human emotions: the natural attraction we feel toward certain people — our friends, for instance — and the equally natural aversion we have toward others. We must expand our sympathies beyond the narrow confines of ego-motivated human feelings, and seek ever more perfectly to live in God's love. This we can do only if we offer ourselves up into the flow of Infinite Love itself.

Moreover, we cannot attain perfection in divine love until we have passed beyond the stage of merely affirming it, and have learned to live in God's actual, loving presence.

Mental belief, in other words, is not enough: We must *experience* God's love. We must channel it consciously to others. We must call it to us with deep faith and devotion. Not only must we pray: We must also, in an uplifted state of soul, *receive* the grace of divine love in our hearts. As St. John wrote: "To all those who *received* him gave he power to become the sons of God."

In inner communion, God enters into the heart, and makes us His own.

Jesus, finally, is speaking of the outward *expression* of perfect love. His words concern not only the inner, ecstatic state of love, but also the manifestation of that selfless, divine love toward others.

We find, then, in these few simple words the very essence of his teaching. What he was saying was, "Seek perfection in God, and give outward expression to what you receive from Him, by universal love for all." To seek God inwardly, and to serve Him outwardly in all: What higher message could God have given to humanity?

In teaching us these truths, God, through the Holy Bible, has spoken to mankind.

Bhagavad Gita

Be Willing To Stand Alone

This passage is from the seventh Chapter, the 3rd Stanza:

"Out of thousands, one strives for spiritual attainment; and out of many blessed true seekers, who strive assiduously to reach Me, one, perhaps, perceives Me as I am."

Commentary

Lest anyone lose courage over the odds that are presented here, it might be well to explain that in God's creation there are many planes of existence, through which the soul must pass on its way to oneness with God. As Jesus put it, "In my Father's house are many mansions." (John 14:2) Few indeed on this earth are spiritually determined enough to surrender everything to God. Ours is a relatively unenlightened planet, darkened by materialism, and kept in constant turmoil by mankind's consuming hunger for ego-glorification.

The Bhagavad Gita, however, counts as blessed in God's eyes all those who earnestly strive to live for Him alone. Nor does the Gita state that one cannot find God while living in a human body. It merely poses the challenge: "If you want to find God, don't delude yourself that the path to Him is easy. The spiritual heights cannot be attained with anything less than total dedication to the Lord."

There is another point to be considered here, one which modern man would do well to heed. For, raised as we are on Twentieth Century democratic principles, we may imagine that anything which the majority of religious believers accept as a true teaching must therefore indeed be true.

How many religions, and how many bodies of believers, imagine themselves justified by the sheer numbers of their adherents! How many, besides, think of themselves as true spokesmen for their own religions merely because there are thousands, or even millions, who agree with them!

The Bhagavad Gita here demolishes any such delusion. So also did Jesus, repeatedly, when he offered high spiritual teachings in the form of parables because most of his listeners were not yet spiritually mature enough to "hear" all that he had to impart.

In any field of endeavor, it is normal for the person who has knowledge to impart not to teach those who are too far below him in their ability or understanding. It would be a waste, for example, for a great pianist to teach simple scales to five-year-olds. A master of the piano normally teaches those who have some hope of becoming professional pianists themselves.

In the spiritual world, also, a great master may indeed speak to the multitudes as well — in the compassionate hope that some of them will receive a certain impetus from him, and that, out of this number, some few will decide to live more fully for God. For such a master to live only to inspire lukewarm conversions would, however, be a waste of the supreme gifts that he has to bestow.

Every great master seeks worthy disciples: those on whom he can confer his supreme spiritual treasures. The highest teachings in every true religion are not for everyone — not for the reason that they exclude anyone, but simply because so few people really want to receive them.

Most seekers want ego-gratification, even when they go to church. They want a teaching that says, "Don't try too hard. After all, you're only human. Be honest, be truthful, and occasionally remember the Lord."

We don't often hear religious teachers telling their congregations to forsake everything in their search for God. Were they to do so, how many of them would even keep their jobs?

The influence of mass attitudes is difficult to resist. Many, even among earnest seekers, lose heart after a few tests and turn back, preferring acceptance by the majority over the voice of their own conscience.

Sri Krishna in this passage of the Bhagavad Gita is trying to help people to break the hypnosis of mass opinion. One who would live truly in God must be willing to stand alone, to be mocked by uncomprehending family members, to be persecuted by those who are, in fact, still children in their own spiritual understanding. As Jesus said when he was crucified: "Forgive them, for they know not what they do."

One who would know God must realize that, just as in physical death we leave behind us everything of this earth and go off alone into the great Beyond, so in the death of the ego, when the soul offers itself wholly into God, one must be willing to enter the divine realms alone, with approval from no one, save only from God Himself.

Thus, through the Bhagavad Gita, God has spoken to mankind.

Index of Scriptural Quotations

This index lists the Scriptural passages quoted in the text, in alphabetical order by scriptural location. The Bible quotations are listed first, followed by those from the Bhagavad Gita. Frequently, the passages have been abbreviated; you can find a more complete quotation in the text. A page number in **boldface** refers to a weekly commentary devoted to that quote.

Bible Quotations

Bhagavad Gita Quotations

Gita VII:19 "...hard the wise Mahatma is to find,
That man who sayeth, 'All is Vasudev!'" **149**

Gita IX:33-34 "...Unto My rest your spirits shall be
guided." **129**

Gita X:11 "Out of My love for them, I, the Divine
within them, set alight in them the radiant lamp
of wisdom..." **61**

Gita XI:8 "'Thou canst not see Me with mortal
eyes'..." **77**

Gita XI:12 "If there should rise suddenly within the
skies, Sunburst of a thousand suns..." **38**

Gita XII:8-11 "For he that laboureth right for love of
Me, Shall finally attain!..." **140**

Gita XV:11 "Seekers of union with the Lord find
Him dwelling in their own hearts..." **113**

Gita XVIII:64-66 "...Give Me thy heart! adore Me!..."
68

A Selection of Other Books
by J. Donald Walters

Crises in Modern Thought: Solutions to the Problem of Meaninglessness. This book probes the discoveries of modern science for their pertinence to lasting human values.

Cities of Light: What Communities Can Accomplish, and the Need for Them in Our Times.

Rays of the Same Light: Parallel Passages, with Commentary, from the Bible and the Bhagavad Gita. (Volumes II and III)

The Art of Supportive Leadership: A Practical Handbook for People in Positions of Responsibility.

Education for Life — a book on childhood education.

The Search — A Young Person's Quest for Understanding. This autobiography is a deeply moving revelation of a poignant search for truth.

Affirmations & Prayers — a collection of 52 spiritual qualities, a discussion of each, with an affirmation and prayer for its realization.

A new series of Daily Thoughts for the Month:

> **Secrets of Happiness**
> **Secrets of Success**
> **Secrets of Persuasion**
> **Secrets of Attracting and Keeping Friends**
> **Secrets of Inner Peace**
> **Secrets of Meditation**

J. Donald Walters lives at Ananda World Brotherhood Village, the spiritual community he founded in 1968. Ananda is one of the most successful intentional communities in the world. For further information about the community or its guest programs, or for a product brochure, please write the publisher, or call 916-292-3065.